Animal Quotations

G. F. Lamb

Illustrated by William Rushton

'There is something wholly likeable about most people who write about animals.'

Eric Duthie

Longman

Longman Group Limited,
Longman House, Burnt Mill, Harlow,
Essex CM20 2JE, England
and Associated Companies throughout the world.

© Longman Group Limited 1985

First published 1985

British Library Cataloguing in Publication Data

Animal quotations.
 1. Zoology
 I. Lamb, G.F.
 591   QL45.2

 ISBN 0-582-89238-4

Set in 9 on 10 point Plantin
by Servis Filmsetting Limited, Manchester

Printed in Great Britain
by Spottiswoode Ballantyne Ltd.,
Colchester & London.

Contents

Contents

Contents

Foreword

Most of us are interested in animals. We keep pets, we visit zoos, we watch animal programmes on television, we read animal books. There are literally hundreds of books dealing with various forms of animal life. Strangely enough, though, there has never, to my knowledge, been a book of quotations about animals. This book is designed to fill the gap.

The quotations have been carefully chosen. A few are short and succinct ('A horse! A horse! my kingdom for a horse!'), but most, though not lengthy, are long enough to be interesting in themselves – informative, descriptive, anecdotal, amusing, or thought-provoking.

There are well over a thousand quotations about animals here, gathered from a wide range of sources and covering a wide range of non-human animals. I have deliberately restricted the book to four-footed beasts and mammals, for this is what most people have in mind when they talk about animals. To have included birds, reptiles, and insects (though these are animals in the broad sense) would have extended the book unduly.

The five main sections into which I have divided the animal kingdom are simply for the reader's convenience. Though not (I hope) scientifically inaccurate – apes and monkeys, for instance, are kept distinct – the divisions are not intended to be scientific, and the dividing lines are far from rigid. Nor should they be taken too literally. 'Animals in the Field' is a section dealing primarily with animals which have been used by man to serve his interests, as distinct from domestic pets or wild animals. 'Field' in this connection includes 'desert', and the camel will be found alongside the cow and the horse.

Again, some animals could have been included equally well in a different section. Elephants at work in their native land are in a sense captive animals. But the element of captivity is far less evident here than when an elephant is performing tricks in a circus. I have therefore preferred to put quotations about working elephants in the section devoted to animals in the wild. Incidentally, it should hardly be necessary to add that an animal in the wild is not necessarily the same as a wild animal. A field-mouse is as much in a state of nature as is a tiger.

Entries are dated where possible according to the date of first publication. However, where the date of *writing* is known to me, this is given instead. Where Gilbert White, for example, has dated a letter, I give this date. Otherwise, I give the date of the first publication of the famous *Natural history of Selborne*.

In general I have preferred to deal with real animals rather than with a fiction writer's creations. Natural historians and poets figure more freely, therefore, than novelists and playwrights. The first-named are obviously drawn upon with particular freedom. Such names as Gilbert White, Richard Jefferies, and W. H. Hudson naturally occur quite often. But there is no league table of writers on natural history. There may be various reasons for the inclusion or omission of a particular writer. The fact that I have included one writer but not another does not necessarily mean that I rate the latter less highly.

It would be foolish to pretend that there is no darker side to the literature of animal life. There are all too many grim, disturbing, and disgraceful passages to be found in books and articles. But my purpose here has been mainly to give pleasure. I have not ignored the black moments, but I have not stressed them. This is a book to be enjoyed. I hope you enjoy it.

G. F. Lamb

The animal world

GETTING ON WITH ANIMALS

Animals are such agreeable friends – they ask no questions, they pass no criticisms.

George Eliot   *Mr Gilfil's love-story*, 1857

To get on with animals you must have a sense of humour.

'Saki' *The unbearable Bassington*, 1912

Animals other than Man tend to be better behaved. They don't get drunk, (or) beat each other up at football matches.

Mike Harding   *The armchair anarchists' almanac*, 1981

I think I could turn and live with animals, they are so placid and self-contained,
I stand and look at them long and long.
They do not sweat and whine about their condition.
They do not lie awake in the dark and weep for their sins.

Walt Whitman   *Song of myself*, 1855

It is no doubt a mistake to attribute to [animals] all human feelings, but equally it is surely a mistake to deny that there is a common thread joining all living creatures.

Jo Grimond   *Daily Telegraph*, 5 Dec. 1983

All animals except man know that the ultimate of life is to enjoy it.

Samuel Butler   *Note books*, 1912

Love the animals: God has given them the rudiments of thought and joy untroubled.

T. M. Dostoyevsky   *The brothers Karamazov*, 1880

A kindly gesture bestowed by us on an animal arouses prodigies of understanding and gratitude.

Colette   *Journey for myself*, 1928

The human conscience has developed considerably in recent years in regard to the treatment both of human beings and of animals, though conscience is frequently dumb in the impressive presence of economic interests.

Robert Lynd   *The book of this and that*, 1915

I really don't think I could consent to go to Heaven if I thought that there were to be no animals there. (*Androcles*)

G. Bernard Shaw   *Androcles and the lion*, 1912

Many years ago when an adored dog died, a great friend, a Bishop, said to me, 'You must always remember that, as far as the Bible is concerned, God only threw the humans out of Paradise!'

Quoted in Bruce Fogle   *Pets and their people*, 1983

The beast that cannot use its tongue is not for that reason without a soul within.

Frederick Bligh Bond   *The gospel of Philip the evangelist*, 1932

MAN AND BEAST

The gulf between us and the brutes
Though deep, seems not too wide.

Louis MacNeice   *Jigsaw III*, 1957

The behaviour of men to the lower animals, and their behaviour to each other, bear a constant relationship.

Herbert Spencer   *Social statics*, 1850

I believe that animals have been talking to human beings ever since we were all made and put into this world.

Barbara Woodhouse   *Talking to animals*, 1954

I believe that our domestic animals were originally chosen by uncivilized men because they were useful.

Charles Darwin   *On the origin of species*, 1859

It must be remembered that dogs, cats, birds, and other pets accomplish much in easing the loneliness of millions of people, and in this way alone serve humanity in no small degree.

Eric Delderfield *Second book of true animal stories*, 1972

Superior as we are, they yet depend
Not more on human help than we on theirs.
Their strength, or speed, or vigilance were given
In aid of our defects.

William Cowper *The task*, 1785

Darwinism teaches us that we have descended immediately from the primates, and, in a secondary degree, from a long series of earlier mammals, and that, therefore, they are 'our brothers'. Physiology informs us that they have the same nerves and sense organs as we, and the same feelings of pleasure and pain.

Ernst Haeckel *The riddle of the universe*, 1900

The animals are our younger brothers and sisters. It is an important part of our responsibilities to help them, and not to retard their development by cruel exploitation of their helplessness.

Lord Dowding Speech in House of Lords, 1957

It is quite incorrect to say that animals live by instinct and human beings by intelligence. The human being arrives in the world like a kitten, a creature ruled entirely by instinct.

Otto Koehler in *Man and animal*, 1968

Everyone who has domesticated some shy creature can testify to the wealth of character which it came to display in the ripening warmth of intimacy.

Colonel E. B. Hamley *Our poor relations*, 1872

We just want to live in harmony with each other. I've trained them simply on encouraging them to trust their human friends.

Tippi Hedren quoted in *Telegraph Sunday Magazine*, 18 Dec. 1983
[Tippi and her husband own an American ranch where they keep nearly 100 wild animals without bars.]

Each animal
By natural instinct taught, spares his own kind;
But man, the tyrant man, revels at large,
Free-booter unrestrain'd, destroys at will
The whole creation, men and beasts his prey.

   William Somerville *Field sports*, 1742

'I've never been able to understand,' [Lettice continued] 'why
people should be so much more nervous about wild animals,
who nearly always run away except when provoked, than
about other human beings, who are so much more dangerous
and vindictive.'

   Elspeth Huxley *The flame trees of Thika*, 1959

When we speak of the ravages that wild animals commit, we
forget that they are usually of our own prompting or creating.
We set to work and cultivate a district and populate it,
driving out or exterminating the natural food of the beasts,
and then fill large spaces with our own helpless 'domestic'
animals. After this, if the wild beasts eat these we exclaim
against them.

   Phil Robinson *The poets' beasts*, 1885

The beasts that roam over the plain,
My form with indifference see;
They are so unacquainted with man
Their tameness is shocking to me.

   William Cowper *Lines supposed to be written by*
   Alexander Selkirk, 1782

[Selkirk was cast away on an uninhabited island in 1704. His
experiences there formed the basis of Defoe's *Robinson
Crusoe*.]

Nature teaches beasts to know their friends.

   William Shakespeare *Coriolanus*, c. 1608

That man I honour and revere
Who, without favour, without fear,
In the great city dares to stand
The friend of every friendless beast.

   H. W. Longfellow *Tales of a wayside inn*, 1863

When we approach an animal with a rifle and thoughts of a
cooking-pot in our minds, that animal grows restless and

suspicious even before we arrive within range of it; but where we have approached the same animal under the same conditions with a camera we have been able to get to close quarters without any difficulty whatever.

C. Court Treatt *Out of the beaten track*, 1930

'Twould ring the bells of heaven
The wildest peal for years,
If Parson lost his senses
And people came to theirs,
And he and they together
Knelt down with angry prayers
For shamed and shabby tigers
And dancing dogs and bears,
And wretched blind pit-ponies,
And little hunted hares.

Ralph Hodgson *The bells of heaven*, 1917

'Man is the only creature that consumes without producing. He does not give milk, he does not lay eggs, he is too weak to pull the plough . . . Yet he is the lord of all the animals.'

George Orwell *Animal farm*, 1945

In his (or her) lifetime the average Briton eats 8 cattle, 36 sheep, 36 pigs, and 550 poultry. Imagine seeing this sizeable herd in a field – and being told that you would have to eat your way through them!

David Jacobs in *RSPCA today*, spring, 1983

Under Tiger-Man's big-hearted teaching we came to call the birds and beasts 'he' and 'she' instead of 'it', to think of animals as living creatures with personalities and foibles of their own; and henceforth we never killed except of necessity.

Julian Duguid *Green hell*, 1931

I have noticed that most men who live in places where game is plentiful acquire a distaste for killing the wild creatures of the jungle . . . It suggests itself to them that the graceful creatures, whose habits they have studied, have as much right to life as they.

W. Somerset Maugham *The gentleman in the parlour*, 1930

ANIMALS KNOW

When handling wild animals, the love of a mother has to come straight from your heart . . . They can sense whether there is sympathy and compassion for them.

Daphne Sheldrick   *My four-footed family*, 1979

Of one thing I have long been utterly convinced: although the animal cannot have any conception of 'medicine', or 'therapy', it so often seems to be able to differentiate between humans who harass, taunt, or tease mindlessly and those who do things, sometimes unpleasant things, with good intentions.

David Taylor   *Next panda, please*, 1982

Animals are so much quicker in picking up our thoughts than we are in picking up theirs. I believe they must have a very poor opinion of the human race.

Barbara Woodhouse   in *Telegraph Sunday Magazine*, 5 Feb. 1984

Sick animals are so long-suffering and silent. I feel guilty for not having more understanding of what they need. Humans ask; their babies yell; but animals just lie looking at you as they wait to die, and you never know whether they are thinking of anything at all.

Joan Ward-Harris   *Creature comforts*, 1979

Their grave eyes are aware of things we little guess or understand.

'B. B.'   *Wild lone*, 1938

ANIMAL WAYS

They know nothing of our hopes, but they also know nothing of our fears; they are subject to death, as we are, but they are not aware of this. Most of them can take care of themselves better than we can, and they make a less evil use of their passions.

C. L. de Montesquieu   *The spirit of the laws*, 1748

There is a wonderful spirit of sociality in the brute creation
. . . Oxen and cows will not fatten by themselves, and it
would be needless to instance sheep, which constantly flock
together.

Gilbert White   *Natural history of Selborne*, 1775

Which one is the leader of a band of wild animals? In many
kinds of animals that go in herds, the leader . . . is usually not
the strongest but an elderly female.

Ernest Thompson Seton   *Krag, the Kootenay ram*,
1929

We men like to see animals courting. It amuses us to see them
thus imitating humanity.

Julian Huxley   *The courtship of animals*, 1934

Music's force can tame the furious beast.

Matthew Prior   *Solomon*, 1718

ENEMIES

Man is a fearsome animal in his own right and is very
properly shunned by the great majority of wild animals.

Michael Boorer   *Wild cats*, 1969

You cannot shoot an animal twice – but you *can* photograph it
twice.

John Maude   quoted in June Kay,   *The thirteenth
moon*, 1970

Hunting for photographs is far more fascinating and
tantalizing than hunting to kill.

C. Court Treatt   *Out of the beaten track*, 1930

Hi! handsome hunting man
Fire your little gun.
Bang! Now the animal
Is dead and dumb and gone,
Nevermore to peep again, creep again, leap again,
Eat or sleep or drink again, Oh, what fun!

Walter de la Mare   *Collected poems*, 1942

A man out of temper does not wait for proofs before feeling that all things, animate and inanimate, are in a conspiracy against him, but at once thrashes his horse or kicks his dog.

George Eliot   *The mill on the floss*, 1860

You need never fear a man who ill-treats animals. He is a coward anyway.

Harry Leat   *Tragic magic*, 1925

There are scientific people, called Naturalists, to whom no sort of creature that can be classified comes amiss as a victim, from a butterfly to a hippopotamus. Armed sometimes with a rifle, sometimes less expensively with a pin, they go into strange lands to collect what they call the 'fauna'.

Colonel E. B. Hamley   *Our poor relations*, 1872

Over the last decade there's been a growing awareness of the roles we have mapped out for animals. The way some areas of farming, allied to science, have turned livestock into genetic freaks has been upsetting both town and country people.

Lynne Edmunds   in *Daily Telegraph*, 18 Nov. 1983

In the present investigation the experimental kitten was given 5,000 electrical shocks to its rear legs . . . The shocks were administered seven days after birth and continued through the next 35 days.

From *Journal of genetic psychology* (1963), quoted in *The unkindest beast*, 1983
[The purpose of the experiment was 'to induce a schizophrenic-like state in kittens'.]

To all the humble beasts there be,
To all the birds on land and sea,
Great Spirit, sweet protection give,
That free and happy they may live.

John Galsworthy   *Collected poems*, 1934

Animals in the home

A British home is nothing without a pet.
  Yvonne Arnaud   in *News Review*, 8 Apr. 1948

Cat

ALOOF COMPANION

Before a cat will condescend
To treat you as a trusted friend,
Some little token of esteem
Is needed, like a dish of cream.
  T. S. Eliot   *Old Possum's book of practical cats*, 1939

When the tea is brought at five o'clock,
And all the neat curtains are drawn with care,
The little black cat with bright green eyes
Is suddenly purring there.
  Harold Monro   *Milk for the cat*, 1914

Cats seem to go on the principle that it never does any harm
to ask for what you want.
  J. W. Krutch   *The twelve seasons*, 1949

Perkins was on the floor, still vibrant, but aloof. His love was
strictly practical, with a view to the morning milk – it was not
to be squandered on anything merely human.
  Sheila Kaye-Smith   *A day in a woman's life*, 1926

I am the cat who walks by himself, and all places are alike to
me.
  Rudyard Kipling   *The cat that walked by himself*,
1902

With cats, some say, one rule is true:
Don't speak till you are spoken to.

   T. S. Eliot   *Old Possum's book of practical cats*, 1939

The cat is the only non-gregarious domestic animal.

   Francis Galton   *Inquiries into human faculty*, 1883

It has been observed of the whole race that though they will
often obey the order 'Come', they absolutely refuse to
entertain the command 'Go'.

   C. J. Cornish   *Animals of to-day*, 1898

Cruel, but composed and bland,
Dumb, inscrutable, and grand,
So Tiberius might have sat
Had Tiberius been a cat.

   Matthew Arnold   *Poor Matthias*, 1882

Philander's a King, a tyrannous King,
And I am his Nubian slave;
I must bring him milk and a pillow of silk,
All things that a cat may crave.

   H. E. Palmer   *Phil, the black Persian*, 1946

Cats find human beings useful domestic animals; we are
permitted to feed them and, occasionally, to entertain them.

   George Mikes   *Tsi-Tsa*, 1978

Cats, those wonderful creatures which have assimilated
themselves so marvellously with our civilization while
retaining all their highly developed feral instincts.

   'Saki'   *Tobermory*, 1912

The cat has disdained, one might almost say, to make herself
generally useful. The dog sought out man and thrust itself
upon him as a companion; but the cat most reluctantly
consented to leave the jungle to become a goddess by the
banks of the Nile.

   H. H. Johnston   *The taming of the wild*, 1910

Jeremy Bentham was very fond of animals, particularly
'pussies' as he called them. He had one whom he was wont to
invite to eat macaroni at his own table . . . When I knew him

[the cat] he bore the name the Reverend Doctor John Langbourne, and he was alike conspicuous for his gravity and his philosophy.

John Bowring *Memoir of Jeremy Bentham*, 1838

AFFECTIONATE FRIEND

Cats, like men, are flatterers.

Walter Savage Landor *Imaginary conversations*, 1824–9

It is needless to spend any time about her loving nature to man, how she flattereth by rubbing her skin against one's legs, how she whurleth with her voice, having as many tunes as turnes, for she hath one voice to beg and complain, another to testify her delight and pleasure.

Edward Topsell *The history of four-footed beasts*, 1607

Louder he purrs and louder,
In one glad hymn of praise
For all the night's adventures,
For quiet restful days.

Alexander Gray *On a cat, ageing*, 1924

I am inclined to believe that kneading is a more subtle expression of pleasure than a purr. A purr is a boisterous acclamation in comparison. The knead, that gentle in and out movement of paws and claws, is a private demonstration of serene ecstasy.

Derek Tangye *Lama*, 1966

Puss was never mourned as you,
Purrer of the spotless hue . . .
And expectant you would stand
Arched, to meet the stroking hand.

Thomas Hardy *Last words to a dumb friend*, 1904

[Dickens] was reading at a small table; suddenly the candle went out. My father, who was much interested in his book, relighted the candle, stroked the cat, who was looking at him pathetically, and continued his reading. A few minutes later he looked up just in time to see puss deliberately put out the

candle with his paw, and then look appealingly at him. Puss
was given the petting he craved.

Mary Dickens (daughter of Charles)   *My father as I
recall him*, 1898

If I let her in and go on writing without taking notice of her,
there is a real demonstration of affection for five minutes. She
purrs, she walks round and round me, she jumps on my lap,
she rubs her head and nose against my chin.

Matthew Arnold   *Notebooks*, 1902
[This is the same cat described on page 10.]

The cat that comes to my window-sill
When the moon looks cold and the night is still . . .
And says, 'I have finished my evening lark,
And I think I can hear a hound-dog bark.
My whiskers are froze 'nd stuck to my chin –
I wish you'd git up and let me in.'

Ben King   *Verses*, 1894

Calvin could content himself for hours at a low window,
looking into the ravine and at the great trees, noting the
smallest stir there. He delighted above all things to
accompany me walking about the garden . . . rolling over on
the turf and exhibiting his delight in a hundred ways.

C. D. Warner   *My summer in a garden*, 1870

All your wondrous wealth of hair,
Dark and fair,
Silken-shaggy, soft and bright
As the clouds and beams of night,
Pays my reverent hand's caress
Back with friendlier gentleness.

A. C. Swinburne   *To a cat*, 1894

A man possessed a cat on which he doted;
So fine she was, so soft, so silky-coated –
Her very mew had beauty.

La Fontaine   *Fables*, 1668

On the top of a log which we sometimes used as a table sat the
black cat, with a very demure expression. Peterkin was gazing
intently into the cat's face, his nose about four inches from it.

'Cat,' said Peterkin, turning his head a little on one side, 'I love you! . . . Don't you love me?'

To this touching appeal the cat said 'Mew', faintly.

R. M. Ballantyne *The coral island*, 1857

Monty would approach where I was sitting, arch his back, claw for a brief second at the chair's fabric, leap up and settle down, then turn his head upwards to me as if he were saying: 'Thank you very much'.

Derek Tangye *A cat in the window*, 1962

CAT AT PLAY

When I play with my cat, who knows whether I do not make her more sport than she makes me?

Montaigne *Apology for Raimond Sebon*, 1603

See the kitten on the wall,
Sporting with the leaves that fall . . .
What intenseness of desire
In her upward eye of fire!
With a tiger-leap half-way
Now she meets the coming prey.

William Wordsworth *The kitten and falling leaves*, 1804

CAT AND MOUSE

Although there is no generally accepted firm date on which the domestic cat arrived in England, in 948 AD Howell the Good (a Welsh king) sold young tabby kittens for a penny each, but after the kitten had caught its first mouse the value rose to twopence.

Gregory Wane in *Animals* (RSPCA), autumn, 1979

Let take a cat, and fostre him wel with milk,
And tendre flesh, and make him couche of silk,
And let him seen a mous go by the wall;
Anon he weyveth milk, and flesh, and all,
And every deyntee that is in that hous,
Swich appetyt hat he to ete a mous.

Geoffrey Chaucer *The maunciples tale*, c. 1386

Some years ago a famous cat,
The pangs of hunger feeling,
Had chanced to catch a fine young mouse,
Who said, as he ceased squealing:
'All genteel folk their faces wash
Before they think of eating!'
And wishing to be thought well-bred
Puss heeded his entreating.

But when she raised her paw to wash,
Chance for escape affording,
The sly young mouse said his good-bye
Without respect to wording.
A feline council met that day
And passed, in solemn meeting,
A law forbidding any cat
To wash till after eating!

Anon.   *Why cats wash after eating*

The number of humble-bees in any district depends in a
great degree on the number of field-mice, which destroy
combs and nests . . . Now the number of mice is largely
dependent on the number of cats; and Mr Newman says:
'Near villages and small towns I have found the nests of
humble-bees more numerous than elsewhere, which I
attribute to the number of cats.'

Charles Darwin   *On the origin of species*, 1859
[Mr H. Newman was an expert on bees.]

CAT AND FISH

There is a propensity belonging to common house-cats that is
very remarkable; I mean their violent fondness for fish,
which appears to be their favourite food . . . for of all
quadrupeds, cats are the least disposed towards water, and
will not, if they can avoid it, deign to wet a foot.

Gilbert White   *Natural history of Selborne*, 1770

One [cat] was an accomplished trout-catcher, in spite of the
Gaelic proverb and universal saying that the cat loves fish but
fears to wet its feet.

W. H. Hudson   *A shepherd's life*, 1910

A whisker first, and then a claw,
With many an ardent wish,
She stretched in vain to reach the prize –
What female heart can gold despise?
What Cat's averse to Fish?

Thomas Gray *On a favourite cat, drowned in a tub of goldfishes,* 1747

'Where is the cat?' said Geraldine. 'The cat!' said Helen [the maid] grimly. 'I have all but killed her with the besom.' 'Why, for goodness sake?' 'Because she ate my red herring! I set it all ready on the end of the dresser, and she ran away with it and ate every morsel to the tail . . .' 'And have you had no dinner?' asked Geraldine. 'Oh yes, I had mutton enough, but I had just set my heart on a red herring.'

   Which was the most deserving of having a besom taken to her, the cat or the woman?

Jane Carlyle *Letters,* 1843

CAT AND BIRD

O cat of churlish kind
The fiend was in thy mind
When thou my bird untwin'd

John Skelton *A curse on a cat,* 1560
[untwin'd = destroyed]

The black cat from the house next door
Waits with death in each bared claw
For the tender unwary bird
That all the summer I have heard
In the orchard singing.

Clifford Dyment *Man and beast,* 1944

They call me cruel. Do I know if mouse or song-bird feels?
I only know they make me light and salutary meals.
And if, as 'tis my nature to, ere I devour I tease 'em,
Why should a low-bred gardener's boy pursue me with a besom?

C. S. Calverley *Sad memories,* 1862

For he will not do destruction if he is well-fed, neither will he spit without provocation.

For he purrs in thankfulness when God tells him he is a good cat.

Christopher Smart   *My cat Jeoffrey*

CAT AND HARE

My friend had a helpless little leveret brought to him, which the servants fed with milk from a spoon, and about the same time that his cat kittened and the young [kittens] were despatched and buried . . . In about a fortnight he observed his cat, with tail erect, trotting towards him, and calling with short inward notes of complacency the leveret that she had been supplying with her milk, and continued to support with great affection.

Gilbert White   *Natural history of Selborne*, 1776

CAT LANGUAGE

Cats seldom have much trouble in expressing their feelings towards us. Some cats talk a lot, but more universally they employ body language, which, with their very expressive faces, can convey almost every known emotion.

J. Kimpton   in *The cat* (CPL)[1], Jan. 1984
[CPL is an abbreviation for Cats Protection League.]

Anyone who claims that a cat cannot give a dirty look either has never kept a cat or is singularly unobservant!

Maurice Burton   *Just like an animal*, 1978

I am not a cat man, but a dog man, and all felines can tell this at a glance – a sharp, vindictive glance.

James Thurber   *Lanterns and lances*, 1961

TAME OR WILD?

He will lie on a rug tomorrow
And lick his silky fur,
And veil the brute in his yellow eyes,
And play he's tame, and purr.

But at midnight in the alley
He will crouch against the wall,
And beat the time for his demon's song
With the swing of his demon's tail.

Don Marquis   *The tomcat*, 1917

The most domestic cat, which has lain on a rug all her days,
appears quite at home in the woods, and, by her sly and
stealthy behaviour, proves herself more native there than the
regular inhabitants.

H.D. Thoreau   *Walden*, 1854

The Australian bush-cat has a nasty, unpleasant habit of
dragging a long, wriggling, horrid, black snake into a room
where there are ladies, proudly laying it down in a
conspicuous place (usually in front of the exit), and then
looking up for approbation. She wonders, perhaps, why the
visitors are in such a hurry to leave.

Henry Lawson   *Up the country*, 1892–4

CATS AND COLOUR

The tortoise-shell cat
She sits on the mat,
As gay as a sunflower she.

Patrick Chalmers   *The tortoise-shell cat*, 1914

As a rule it is the females alone in cats which are tortoise-
shell, the corresponding colour in the males being rusty-red.

Charles Darwin   *The descent of man*, 1901

It is the distinction of the black cat that he is one of the few
cheerful superstitions left to us.

Robert Lynd   *The book of this and that*, 1915

He is a grey, white-chested cat,
And barred with black along the grey;
Not large, and the reverse of fat,
His profile good from either way.

Roy Fuller   *The family cat*, 1962

Every cat in the twilight's grey,
Every possible cat.

Patrick Chalmers   *The tortoise-shell cat*, 1914

Cats with blue eyes are invariably deaf.

Charles Darwin *On the origin of species*, 1859

Many [Blue-eyed cats] were found to be deaf . . . In attempts to breed out this distressing condition . . . the Orange-eyed White was produced, happily possessed of perfect hearing.

Angela Sayer in *The colourful world of cats*, 1975

I have possessed both stone-deaf white cats and a blue Persian. Although deaf to ordinary sounds, they would invariably jump on top of the piano when it was played.

Louis Wain (famous cat artist) in *Daily Mail*, 25 Jan. 1916

Johnny is a long-haired Blue,
Looks a gentleman to you.
But his Ma was black and white,
Loved a dustbin, loved a fight.

Ruth Pitter *Three cheers for the black, white and blue*, 1947

CAT UP A TREE

Sometimes ascending, debonair,
An apple-tree or lofty pear,
Lodg'd with convenience in the fork,
She watch'd the gardener at his work.

William Cowper *The retired cat*, 1791

I have never understod this particular blind spot of cats, how time and again they will climb to inaccessible places with the greatest of ease, then become transfixed with the height they have reached.

Derek Tangye *A cat in the window*, 1962

The boy climbed up into the tree.
The tree rocked. So did he.
He was trying to rescue a cat,
A cushion of a cat, from where it sat
In a high crutch of branches, mewing.

Hal Summers

I see her weight as the branch dips
But it has become mine too.

I look both up at her and
Down with her. I dread falling.

Patricia Beer   *The cat in the tree*, 1971

UNLOVED AND STRAY CATS

She had a name among the children;
But no one loved though someone owned
Her, locked her out of doors at bedtime
And had her kittens duly drowned.

Edward Thomas   *A cat*, 1920

On coming close to one of these [stray] cats he invariably
looks at you with wide-open startled eyes, and so long as you
stand quietly regarding him he will keep this look. The
moment you speak kindly to him the alarm vanishes from his
eyes, he knows you for a friend, and is as ready as any
starving human beggar to tell you his miserable story.

W. H. Hudson   *Birds in London*, 1898

A condition of the foundation document [of the Mosque of
Sultan Osman] is that stray cats should be fed at the gate, and
this is still the custom.

G. Goodwin   *Islamic architecture, Ottoman Turkey*,
1971

FANATICS AND FELINES

At Aix in Provence on the festival of Corpus Christi the finest
Tom-cat in the country, wrapped like a child in swaddling
clothes, was publicly exhibited in a magnificent shrine . . . In
short, the cat on this occasion was treated like a god.

C. Mills   *History of the Crusades*, 1820

In Anatolia [Asia Minor] the greatest misfortune that can
befall a dead person is for a cat to jump over or upon his
coffin. If this happens the body will not decompose, and the
deceased would thus be prevented from entering Paradise.

William J. Fielding   *Strange superstitions and
magical practices*, 1945

Cats have always figured prominently in superstition and were venerated in ancient Egypt.

Raymond Lamont Brown   *A book of superstitions*, 1970

Martin le Franc, writing about 1440, said the Devil appeared at the sabbat in the shape of a cat, which all the witches worshipped.

Richard Cavendish   *The black arts*, 1967

Elizabeth Francis learned this arte of witchcraft of hyr grandmother. When shee taughte it her, she counseiled her to renounce God and to geue of her bloudde to Sathan, whyche she delyuered her in the lykenesse of a whyte spotted Catte.

Thomas Cooper   *Witches at Chelmsford*, 1617

Frances Moore said that the goodwife Elizabeth Weed gave her a white Cat, telling her that if she would deny God, and affirme the same by her bloud, then whomsoever she cursed and sent that Cat unto, they should dye shortly after.

John Davenport   *Witches of Huntingdon*, 1646

Among other powers attributed to witches was that of turning *themselves* into cats – real cats! In this manner the cat eventually became the symbol of the witch.

J. W. Wickwar   *Witchcraft and the black art*, 1925

KINDNESS TO CATS

Mrs Crupp had indignantly assured him that there wasn't room to swing a cat there: but as Mr Dick justly observed to me . . . 'You know, Trotwood, I don't *want* to swing a cat. I never do swing a cat.'

Charles Dickens   *David Copperfield*, 1849–50

One of Kendell's major projects during the past few years has been a campaign to persuade lexicographers to drop or change the definition of the word 'catty' – currently defined as 'slyly malicious, spiteful'. Kendell considers this an insult to all cats, whom he describes as 'loyal to their last breath'.

Berkeley Rice   *The other end of the leash*, 1968

Mahomet, rather than disturb his cat, which was asleep on it, cut off the skirt of his robe.

Phil Robinson   *The poets' beasts*, 1885

I shall never forget the indulgence with which Dr Johnson treated Hodge, his cat, for whom he himself used to go out and buy oysters lest the servants, having that trouble, should take a dislike to the poor creature.

James Boswell   *Life of Johnson*, 1791

An old bachelor in the parish of Winterborne Bishop had an excessive fondness for cats, and always kept eleven of these animals as pets . . . They had to be fed at the proper time, in their own dining-room, eating their meals from a row of eleven plates on a long, low table made expressly for them.

W. H. Hudson   *A shepherd's life*, 1910

She (my wife) used the old wives' recipe for keeping a cat at home by buttering his paws; the theory being of course that the cat licks off the butter and says to himself that such a nice taste is worth staying for.

Derek Tangye   *A cat in the window*, 1962

O my beloved come again, come back in joy, come back in pain,
To end our searching with a mew, or with a purr our grieving;
And you shall have for lunch or tea whatsoever fish swim in the sea.

E. V. Rieu   *The lost cat*, 1933

QUEER CATS

The cat vanished quite slowly, beginning with the end of the tail, and ending with the grin, which remained some time after the rest of it had gone.

'Well, I've often seen a cat without a grin,' thought Alice; 'but a grin without a cat! It's the most curious thing I ever saw in all my life!'

Lewis Carroll   *Alice's adventures in wonderland*, 1865

Dr Samuel Johnson & his Cat.

Cats no less liquid than their shadows
Offer no angles to the wind.
They slip, diminished, neat, through loopholes
Less than themselves.

A. J. S. Tessimond   *Cats*, 1934

Last night our young cat did leap down our stairs from top to bottom at two leaps, and frighted us, that we could not well tell whether it was the cat or a spirit.

Samuel Pepys   *Diary*, 1667

Cats sleep   Top of piano,
Anywhere,   Window-ledge,
Any table,   In the middle,
Any chair.   On the edge.

Eleanor Farjeon   *Cats*, 1957

Dog

Love me, love my dog.

St Bernard   *Sermon*, c. 1155

Every dog has his day.

George Borrow   *Lavengro*, 1851

THE FRIEND OF MAN

Histories are more full of examples of the fidelity of dogs than of men.

Alexander Pope   *Letters*, 1737

If you pick up a starving dog and make him prosperous he will not bite you. This is the principal difference between a dog and a man.

Mark Twain   *What is man?*, 1906

Say something idiotic and nobody but a dog politely wags his tail.

Virginia Graham   *Everything's too something*, 1966

The great pleasure of a dog is that you may make a fool of yourself with him and not only will he not scold you, but he will make a fool of himself too.

Samuel Butler   *Notebooks*, 1911

23

Dogs laugh, but they laugh with their tails.

Max Eastman quoted in **Bruce Fogle, *Pets and their people*, 1983**

Dogs wave tails or plumes, according to breed, in several indicative ways. There is the wide sweep of expectancy, or the more vigorous movement of greeting. Or, tail under tummy, a subterranean waggle which can be pleasure tinged with guilt or fear.

Elma Williams *The Pant Glas story*, 1970

They are superior to human beings as companions. They do not quarrel or argue with you. They never talk about themselves but listen to you while you talk about yourself, and keep up an appearance of being interested in the conversation.

J. K. Jerome *Idle thoughts of an idle fellow*, 1889

The Dog toils not, neither does he spin, yet Solomon in all his glory never lay upon a doormat all day long, sun-soaked and fly-fed and fat, while his master worked for the means wherewith to purchase an idle wag of the Solomonic tail.

Ambrose Bierce *The devil's dictionary*, 1911

Most dogs love car riding but to Sam it was a passion that never waned – even in the night hours. He would gladly leave his basket when the world was asleep . . . and follow me out into the cold. He would be on the seat before I got the car door fully open.

James Herriot *Vet in harness*, 1974

Beauty travelled in her own compartment in her master's private railroad car in the United States. Her bedroom, furnished with a dog-sized settee and a miniature porcelain bathtub, adjoined Lafayette's in his London town house in Tavistock Square. A plaque on one wall proclaimed, 'The more I see of men, the more I love my dog'.

Milbourne Christopher *The illustrated history of magic*, 1973
[Lafayette was an American illusionist of the early twentieth century.]

The gamekeeper, with dogs around him from morning till night, has no doubts on the matter whatever, but with characteristic decision is perfectly certain that they think and reason in the same way as human beings, though of course in a limited way.

Richard Jefferies   *The gamekeeper at home*, 1878

Scott always talked to Camp [his dog] as if he understood what was said – and the animal certainly did understand not a little of it; it seemed as if he perfectly comprehended that his master considered him as a sensible and steady friend.

J. G. Lockhart   *Life of Sir Walter Scott*, 1838

'A dog must be wooed quite as much as a human being. But my husband won't take any pains with them at all. He expects them all to love him at sight, and if they don't he gets cross with them.'

E. V. Lucas   *Mr Ingleside*, 1910

I have caught more ills from people sneezing over me and giving me virus infections than from kissing dogs.

Barbara Woodhouse   *Telegraph Sunday Magazine*, 5 Feb. 1984

The poor dog, in life the firmest friend,
The first to welcome, foremost to defend,
Whose honest heart is still his master's own,
Who labours, fights, lives, breathes for him alone,
Unhonour'd falls, unnoticed all his worth,
Denied in heaven the soul he held on earth.
While man, vain insect! hopes to be forgiven,
And claims himself a sole exclusive heaven.

Lord Byron   *Inscription on the monument of a Newfoundland dog*, 1808

The dog, which still was hovering nigh,
Repeating the same timid cry,
This dog had been through three months' space
A dweller in that savage place.
Yes, proof was plain that, since the day
When this ill-fated traveller died,
The dog had watched about the spot,
Or by his master's side.

William Wordsworth   *Fidelity*, 1805
[Wordsworth is telling the true story of a tragedy in the Cumbrian mountains.]

A DOG'S LIFE

I do not think that the dog minded poor Mary's plainness.
His dislike arose more probably from the certainty that she
would always stroke him the wrong way, would poke her
fingers into his defenceless eyes, would try to drag him to her
sharp, razor-edged knees.

Hugh Walpole *Jeremy and Hamlet*, 1923

What kind of a life a dog, even a big dog, acquires, I have
sometimes tried to imagine by kneeling or lying full length on
the ground and looking up. The world then becomes
strangely incomplete: one sees little but legs.

E. V. Lucas *One day and another*, 1909

A VARIETY OF BREEDS

My Alsatian Tito . . . knew, by 'telepathy', exactly which
people got on my nerves, and when. Nothing could prevent
her from biting, gently but surely, all such people on their
posteriors.

Konrad Lorenz *King Solomon's ring*, 1952

I once saw an Alsatian give himself a cooling drink of water
from a tap set in the wall near the quayside at Weymouth. By
standing on his hind legs and steadying himself with one paw
on the wall he was able to press down on the top of the tap
with the other paw, thereby turning it on.

J. G. Rees letter in *Daily Telegraph*, 27 Aug. 1983

I am the dog world's best detective.
My sleuthing nose is so effective
I sniff the guilty at a distance,
And then they lead a doomed existence.

Edward Anthony *The bloodhound*

In a minute or two a large bulldog was seen bounding along
the orchard to his master. 'Mark him, Caesar,' said the
farmer to the dog. 'Mark him.' The dog crouched down on
the grass with his head up and eyes glaring at Jack.

Captain F. Marryat *Mr Midshipman Easy*, 1836
[Jack is up a tree in the farmer's orchard.]

Bull-terriers are curious dogs, and one has to be a little kinky to like them. The majority of people, unfortunately, regard them as ruthless killers and a disgrace to the canine world.

June Kay *The thirteenth moon*, 1970

Greyhounds are pure carnivores. When they chase the hare at a race it's not for fun – they literally want to tear it to pieces.

Phil Rees (greyhound trainer)   quoted in *Radio Times*, 28 June 1980

A cross with a greyhound has given a whole family of shepherd-dogs a tendency to hunt hares.

Charles Darwin *On the origin of species*, 1859

Though Man, for centuries of care,
Has taught the Hound to hunt the Hare,
It's not a natural pursuit,
For each was born a kindly brute.

A. P. Herbert *Silver stream*, 1962

My beautiful white greyhound, Mayflower, is as whimsical as the finest lady in the land. Amongst her other fancies, she has taken a violent affection for a most hideous stray dog who made his appearance here about six months ago . . . made him sharer of her bed and of her mess; and finally established him as one of the family.

M. R. Mitford *Our village*, 1819

All labradors look rather friendly and pleased with themselves and with the world at large. Labradors acting as guides (for the blind) look not only pleased but confident, patient, and slightly self-important.

Jo Grimond *Daily Telegraph*, 5 Dec. 1983

This island of England breeds very valiant creatures: their mastiffs are of unmatchable courage.

William Shakespeare *Henry V*, 1599

Outside her kennel the mastiff old
Lay fast asleep, in moonlight cold.
The mastiff old did not awake,
Yet she an angry moan did make.

S. T. Coleridge *Christabel*, 1816

A mastiff dog
May love a puppy cur for no more reason
Than that the twain have been tied up together.

Alfred Tennyson *Queen Mary*, 1875

Under the arch of the South Bridge is a huge mastiff,
sauntering down the middle of the causeway as if with his
hands in his pockets: he is old, grey, brindled, as big as a little
Highland bull.

Dr John Brown *Rab and his friends*, 1859

'It's Carlo, my mastiff . . . We feed him once a day, and not
too much then, so that he is always as keen as mustard.
Toller, my groom, lets him loose every night, and God help
the trespasser he lays his fangs upon.'

A. Conan Doyle *The copper beeches*, 1892

I had a mastiff myself once, which would not suffer any man
to bring in his weapon further than my gate; neither those
that were of my house to be touched in his presence.

William Harrison *Elizabethan England*, 1577

As a small boy I could always make friends at once with any
animal . . . When I was five I was found in a kennel with a
ferocious bull mastiff. We had only had him for a short time,
and the adults, who thought he was vicious, were horrified.

Buster Lloyd-Jones *The animals came in one by
one*, 1966

Pekes
Are biological freaks.

E. B. White *Fashions in dogs*, 1928

For one shilling spectators could witness a poodle solving
simple sums with numbered cards, spelling out the answers
to questions they posed, distinguishing colours, playing
dominoes, and finding selected cards.

Edwin A. Dawes *The great illusionists*, 1979
[The poodle, Munito, was shown in London in 1817.]

Charley [French poodle] was born on the outskirts of Paris
and trained in France, and while he knows a little poodle-

English, he responds quickly only to commands in French. Otherwise he has to translate, and that slows him down.

John Steinbeck *Travels with Charley*, 1962

Poodles always listen attentively while being scolded, looking innocent, bewildered, and misunderstood.

James Thurber *Lanterns and lances*, 1961

When I drove into the stable-yard, Linda (the St Bernard) was greatly excited, weeping profusely, and throwing herself on her back that she might caress my foot with her great fore-paws.

Charles Dickens quoted in **John Forster**, *Life of Charles Dickens*, 1872–4

No man had a more thorough knowledge of where good liquor might be produced for Watch and himself – Watch, like other good sheepdogs, being accustomed to live chiefly on bread and beer.

M. R. Mitford *Our village*, 1819

When the sheep were feeding quietly and there was little or nothing to do for hours at a time, he would not lie down and go to sleep like any other sheepdog, but would spend his vacant time 'amusing of hisself' on some smooth slope where he could roll over and over; then run back and roll over again and again, playing by himself just like a child.

W. H. Hudson *A shepherd's life*, 1910

A whole pack of wild dogs will scarcely ever venture to attack a flock of sheep guarded by even one of these faithful sheepdogs . . . It ranks the sheep as its fellow brethren and thus gains confidence; and the wild dogs, though knowing that individual sheep are good to eat, yet partly consent to this view when seeing them in a flock with a shepherd-dog at their head.

Charles Darwin *Zoology of the voyage of the 'Beagle'*, 1840

Half the handsome spaniels in England are called Dash, just as half the tall footmen are called Thomas.

M. R. Mitford *Our village*, 1819

Over the level the terrier speeds and springs,
Hoping to catch the swallows in their low swift rings.
  Edmund Blunden   *Village sketch*, 1937

Mr Mitchell, the comedian, had given Dickens a small white
shaggy terrier who bore at first the imposing name of Timber
Doodle.
  John Forster   *Life of Charles Dickens*, 1872–4

Timber has had every hair upon his body cut off because of
the fleas, and he looks like the ghost of a drowned dog come
out of a pond after a week or so. It is awful to see him slide
into a room. He is always turning round and round to look for
himself.
  Charles Dickens   quoted in **Forster's** *Life of Dickens*,
1872–4
[Fortunately, in due course, the dog recovered.]

BARKING AND BITING

Let dogs delight to bark and bite
For God hath made them so.
  Isaac Watts   *Divine songs for children*, 1715

What delight can there be, and not rather displeasure, in
hearing the barking and howling of dogs?
  Thomas More   *Utopia*, 1516

Cowardly dogs bark loudest.
  John Webster   *The white devil*, 1612

On moony nights the dogs bark shrill
Down the valley and up the hill.
  Frances Cornford   *Night song*, 1915

'Nothing makes a dog madder,' said Mitchell, 'than to have
another dog come outside his fence and sniff and bark at him
through the cracks when he can't get out.'
  Henry Lawson   *Mitchell*, 1895

I am driven mad by dogs, who have taken it into their
accursed heads to assemble every morning in the piece of
ground opposite, and who have barked this morning for five

hours without intermission; positively rendering it
impossible for me to work.

Charles Dickens   *Letters*, 1898

It follows not, because
The hair is rough, the dog's a savage one.

J. Sheridan Knowles   *The daughter*, 1836

The owner of a dangerous Doberman Pinscher offered
Windermere magistrates a spirited mitigation after the animal
had bitten the leg of a passer-by. 'The dog is a pet, a great big
soft dog. It often walks past people without biting them.'

Daily Telegraph, 15 Dec. 1983

Dogs were a Stuart family weakness, and one Cavalier, who
had the misfortune of being bitten, could not refrain from the
complaint: 'God bless your Majesty but God damn your
dogs!'

Christopher Falkus   *Charles II*, 1972

You have killed the tiny bird
Which flew not till today,
Against my orders, whom you heard
Forbidding you the prey.

'Sir, when I flew to seize the bird
In spite of your command,
A louder voice than yours I heard,
And harder to withstand.
You cried – Forbear! – but in my breast
A mightier cried – Proceed! –
'Twas Nature, Sir, whose strong behest
Impelled me to the deed.'

William Cowper   *On a spaniel called Beau, killing a
young bird*, and *Beau's reply*, 1793

I'm a lean dog, a keen dog, a wild dog, and lone;
I'm a rough dog, a tough dog, hunting on my own;
I'm a bad dog, a mad dog, teasing silly sheep;
I love to sit and bay the moon to keep fat souls from sleep.

Irene Macleod   *Lone dog*, 1915

Many people say that there are no bad dogs, only bad owners.
The basis for that is true, but it is not a law of the universe.
There *are* bad dogs; bad in the sense that they are unsuitable
as family pets.

Bruce Fogle   *Pets and their people*, 1983

The dog and man at first were friends;
But when a pique began,
The dog, to gain some private ends,
Went mad, and bit the man . . .

The man recovered of the bite,
The dog it was that died.

Oliver Goldsmith   *The vicar of Wakefield*, 1761

PLAYING THE CLOWN

The usual dog about the Town
Is much inclined to play the clown.

T. S. Eliot   *Old Possum's book of practical cats*, 1939

Montmorency's ambition in life is to get in the way and be
sworn at. If he can squirm in anywhere where he is
particularly not wanted, and be a perfect nuisance, and make
people mad, and have things thrown at his head, then he feels
his day has not been wasted.

J. K. Jerome   *Three men in a boat*, 1889
[Montmorency is a small fox terrier of innocent
appearance.]

She would fly up to you and, where any other dog would have
slowed down and stopped, she would go right on, bowling
you over and racing on without any reduction in speed. She
was a born hit-and-run driver.

Buster Lloyd-Jones   *The animals came in one by
one*, 1966

He took sinewy lumps from the shins of old frumps,
And mangled the errand boys – when he could get 'em.
He shammed furious rabies, and bit all the babies,
And followed the cats up the trees, and then ate 'em.

Rupert Brooke   *The little dog's day*, 1907

I cannot say he was a good house-dog, for he had a curious habit of barking only at his friends. Strangers he treated with silent contempt.

Angelo Lewis *Conjurer Dick*, 1886

On one occasion a dog which was supposed to be playing the piano allowed itself to be lured away by a sausage thrown on the stage by one of the spectators . . . The piano went on playing just the same.

Hermann Dembeck *Willingly to school*, 1970

A WORLD OF SMELLS

We see . . . how he is at once in a world of smells of which we know nothing, which so occupy and absorb his attention as to make him practically blind to everything about him and deaf to all sounds, even of his master's voice impatiently calling him.

W. H. Hudson *A hind in Richmond Park*, 1922

They haven't got no noses,
The fallen sons of Eve . . .
And goodness only knowses
The Noselessness of Man.

G. K. Chesterton *Song of Quoodle*, 1914

The bitch alternately sniffed at the surfaces popular in canine society and made its own contribution to The Dog's World, that archetype of the wall newspaper.

A. Calder-Marshall *The magic of my youth*, 1951

DOG TEAMS

Two things that proved very helpful to Amundsen in the attainment of the South Pole were his favourable base and his excellent dogs.

Vihljamur Stefansson *Great adventures and explorations*, 1947

There are few sights as impressive as a fresh dog team in full cry: the dogs are so obviously happy, and happiness is always inspiring. They . . . gallop along apparently quite unconscious of the sledge behind.

J. M. Scott *The land that God gave Cain*, 1933

The more you drive dogs, the more, I think, you enjoy it.

   Martin Lindsay   *Those Greenland days*, 1932

It is always hard to make the dogs leap a widening crack,
though some of the best dog-drivers can do it instantly, using
the whip and the voice.

   Robert E. Peary   *The North Pole*, 1910
   [Peary was the first man to reach the North Pole – 1909.]

December 2, 1910. It blew very hard, and the sea got up . . .
Occasionally a heavy sea would bear one of the dogs away,
and he was saved only by his chain. One was washed away
with such force that his chain broke, and he disappeared
overboard. The next wave miraculously washed him on
board again.

   Captain R. F. Scott   *Last journal*, 1923

A HEART TO TEAR

Brothers and sisters, I bid you beware
Of giving your heart to a dog to tear.

   Rudyard Kipling   *The power of the dog*, 1909

It is strange how we buy our sorrow
For the touch of perishing things, idly, with open eyes:
How we give our hearts to brutes that will die in a few
seasons.

   J. C. Squire   *A dog's death*, 1926

Near this spot
Are deposited the remains of one
Who possessed Beauty without Vanity
Strength without Insolence
Courage without Ferocity
And all the Virtues of Man without his Vices.
This praise, which would be unmeaning Flattery
If inscribed over human ashes,
Is but a just tribute to the Memory of
     BOATSWAIN, a Dog.

   Lord Byron   *Inscription on the tomb of his*
   Newfoundland dog, 1808

Now thou art dead, no eye shall ever see,
For shape and service, Spaniell like to thee.

This shall my love doe, give thy sad death one
Teare, that deserves of me a million.

Robert Herrick   *Hesperides*, 1648

Mouse

Not a mouse
Shall disturb this hallow'd house.

William Shakespeare   *A midsummer night's dream*,
c. 1595

A mouse in the wainscot scratches, and scratches, and then
There is no sound at the top of the house, of men
Or mice.

John Drinkwater   *Moonlit apples*, 1923

The mouse
Finds no pleasure in a poor man's house.

Francis Quarles   *Emblems*, 1635

The mouse that hath but one hole is quickly taken.

George Herbert   *Jacula Prudentium*, 1651

She was so charitable and so pitous
She wolde wepe if that she sawe a mouse
Caught in a trappe, if it were dead or bledde.

Geoffrey Chaucer   *The Canterbury tales*, c. 1388

I remembered how Great-Aunt Anne, who wouldn't have a
trap or poison in her farm home, left a plate with crumbs on
the kitchen floor, and shreds of soft wool or cotton near it. 'If
they have food and something for nests, they don't need to
bother anything else.'

Helen Hoover   *A place in the woods*, 1970

I think mice
Are rather nice.

Rose Fyleman   *Mice*

It is an engaging problem in ethics whether, if you have been
lent a cottage, you have the right to feed the mice.

Robert Lynd   *The peal of bells*, 1924

In some farmhouses they still use the ancient lanterns made of tin – huge machines intended for a tallow candle . . . These lanterns are hung up to a beam in the kitchen. Sometimes they are found to be swinging to and fro, and partly turning round. A mouse has got in – for the grease. But how?

Richard Jefferies   *The gamekeeper at home*, 1878

When I was building, one of these [mice] had a nest underneath the house, and . . . would come out regularly at lunch time and pick up the crumbs at my feet. It probably had never seen a man before, and it soon became quite familiar, and would run over my shoes and up my clothes.

H. D. Thoreau   *Walden*, 1854

We tried feeding him on many things: rolled oats, powdered milk, Roman meal, soup powder, and birdseed. The one thing he would not eat was cheese.

Harold Horwood   *The foxes of Beachy Cove*, 1967
[This was a forest mouse, rescued from apparent death.]

Here where the Vicar never looks
I nibble through old service books.
Lean and alone I spend my days
Behind this Church of England baize.

John Betjeman   *Diary of a church mouse*, 1954

The brisk Mouse may feast her selfe with crumbs
Till that the green-ey'd Kitling comes.
Then to her Cabbin, blest she can escape
The sudden danger of a Rape.

Robert Herrick   *Hesperides (A country-life)*, 1648

A Mouse that prayed for Allah's aid
Blasphemed when no such aid befell:
A Cat, who feasted on that mouse,
Thought Allah managed vastly well.

'Saki'   *For the duration of the war*, 1915

For one whole year the dove had a companion and daily visitor – a little mouse that used to come and feed with it. The dove would carry it and cover it over with her wings, and make loving noises to it.

Dorothy Wordsworth   *Journal*, 1802

Ah mice, rejoice! Ye've lost your foe,
Who watch'd your scheming robb'ries so
That, while she lived, twa'nt yours to know
A crumb of bread:
'Tis yours to triumph, mine's the woe,
Now pussy's dead.

John Clare

What do we do if the cat brings in a live rodent? . . . The opening of a well-placed gumboot, laid horizontally on the floor, can provide an irresistible bolt-hole for an intelligent mouse . . . He can then be transported to a safe place.

Richard D. Ryder in *Animals* (RSPCA), autumn, 1979

Pleasing and peculiar pets

Bill [Badger] often came inside with the family. But only under supervision. If he heard a spring creak he'd think nothing of ripping a chair side clean out with his powerful claws.

Phil Drabble *A weasel in my meatsafe*, 1977

Once in Canada when I was up in the woods in Northern Quebec I came across a settlement where the innkeeper had a tame black bear running about the place.

Thomas Firbank *I bought a mountain*, 1940

You cannot keep a fully grown chimpanzee in the house. If he decides to throw himself at you out of affection he can easily knock you down the stairs. They also become unpredictable and lose their tempers for no apparent reason, and are capable of causing considerable damage around the house.

Terry Murphy *Some of my best friends are animals*, 1979

If a ferret bites you it is nearly always your own fault. Almost certainly it is from fear, because you have not handled him enough to gain his confidence.

Phil Drabble *Pleasing pets*, 1975

He took up his abode with his two ferrets, harmless, foreign-looking things (no native English animal has so outlandish an appearance as the ferret, with its long limber body, its short legs, red eyes, and ermine-looking fur), of whose venom he was wont to boast.

M. R. Mitford   *Our village*, 1824–32

There is a market for live fox cubs. They are bought and reared as pets. They become quite tame, and will grow up to be friendly with dogs.

Thomas Firbank   *I bought a mountain*, 1940

The gentle and caressing way in which it [a gibbon ape] clasps me round the neck with its long arms, laying its head on my chest, and watching my face with its dark brown eyes, uttering a satisfied crooning sound, is most engaging.

H. O. Forbes   *Handbook to the primates*, 1894

The young gorilla was romping and rolling in full liberty about the private drawing-room, now looking out of the window with becoming gravity and sedateness, as though thoroughly interested in the busy multitude outside; then bounding rapidly along on knuckles and feet to examine and poke fun at some newcomer.

The Times, 1910

Cavies or guinea-pigs make beautifully tame and gentle pets . . . The Dutch are said to have brought them to this country about two centuries ago from their colony Guiana, in South America, from which they are supposed to have got their popular name.

Phil Drabble   *Pleasing pets*, 1975

When Watch [a sheepdog] first saw these pets [guinea-pigs] he was very much attracted . . . David one day consented to take them out and put them on the grass in the dog's presence. In a surprisingly short time they made the discovery that this particular dog was not an enemy but a playmate. He rolled on the grass among them and chased them round and round . . . and they appeared to think it was very good fun.

W. H. Hudson   *A shepherd's life*, 1910

While we were at supper a voice on the outside of the parlour inquired if one of my [pet] hares had got away. I immediately rushed into the next room, and found that my poor favourite Puss had made her escape. She had gnawed the strings of a lattice work with which I thought I had sufficiently secured the window . . . She ran right through the town . . . The poor creature received only a little hurt in one of her claws and one of her ears, and is now almost as well as ever.

   William Cowper   *Letters*, 1780

A Turkey carpet was his lawn,
Whereon he loved to bound,
To skip and gambol like a fawn,
And swing his rump around.

   William Cowper   *Epitaph on a hare*, 1784

In India Colonel Sykes possessed a hyena cub, which was allowed to run about the house. On the voyage home it played with the sailors, as playful and good-humoured as a puppy.

   Proceedings of the Zoological Society, 1833

The lamb while from her hand he thus his supper took
Seemed to feast with head and ears; his tail with pleasure shook.
'Drink, pretty creature, drink,' she said in such a tone
That I almost received her heart into my own.

   William Wordsworth   *The pet lamb*, 1800

'I've never trodden on a pet lamb,' said Lady Caroline, 'so I've no idea what its behaviour would be under the circumstances.'

   'Saki'   *The unbearable Bassington*, 1912

The young leopard always chose to be hungry at night. It howled so pitifully and with such a loud voice that its mistress was obliged to get up and feed this ravenous creature with warm milk, sucked out of a sponge.

   J. G. Wood   *Glimpses into petland*, 1863

The Sangers possess lions at the present day, and one of them is so tame that, as I am informed, it is allowed to roam at large in their house, like a domestic tabby.

   Thomas Frost   *Circus life and circus celebrities*, 1875

It is no use adopting a monkey unless you are prepared to give him nearly as much care as a baby to make him feel that he is one of the family.

Helen M. Sidebotham *Mysteries of the zoo*, 1927

Their social habits, sanitary habits, and very intelligence preclude monkeys from ever being good pets. First of all, monkeys have terrible toilet habits – terrible to us, that is . . . They are almost impossible to house train.

Bruce Fogle *Pets and their people*, 1983

Mij seemed to regard me closely as I composed myself on my back with a cushion under my head; then with a confiding air of knowing exactly what to do, he clambered up beside me and worked his body down into the sleeping-bag until he lay flat on his back inside it with his head on the cushion beside mine.

Gavin Maxwell *A ring of bright water*, 1960
[Mij is a tame otter.]

A gardener of peculiar taste
On a young hog his favour placed;
With other pigs it did not roam,
But fed within its master's home;
He fondly stroked it every day
And taught it all a puppy's play.
No matter where he went, the hog
Followed behind him, like a dog.

John Gay *Fables*, 1727 (modernized)

Of all animals, rabbits are those that boys are most fond of. They are extremely pretty, nimble in their movements, engaging in their attitudes, and always completely under immediate control.

William Cobbett *Cottage economy*, 1822

I have had rabbits of every imaginable breed, and of no breed at all; and although I could make but little way with the old ones, I used to render the young so tame that they would scramble upon my knees as I sat on the grass, and take bread from my hands.

J. G. Wood *Glimpses into petland*, 1863

For the rat collectively I have not a good word to say . . . but as to Samuel Whiskers personally, I can but testify that I have seldom met a more charming and lovable creature. He won all hearts, and everyone was devoted to him.

   Frances Pitt   *Friends of fur and feather*, 1946

The dogs rolled over on the grass, wrestled, and chased their tails. Benjamin [a sheep] stood looking puzzled but willing to learn. Before the week was out he thought he was a dog too, and the dogs accepted him as one of themselves.

   Buster Lloyd-Jones   *The animals came in one by one*, 1966

Surprising as it may seem, the typical skunk, especially when captured young, is said to make a pretty and agreeable pet, gentle in manners and cleanly in its habits; while the beauty of its fur makes it appear highly attractive.

   Harmsworth natural history, 1910

I found Kay standing on a chair in the kitchen with the stoat staring up at her, menacingly. For some reason the stoat seemed to have taken a deep dislike to her. As soon as I called him he came trotting over to me as pally as a puppy dog.

   Terry Murphy   *Some of my best friends are animals*, 1979

The weasel was so tame that he could walk about anywhere he liked with it in his pocket and it would never try to escape. It would simply run up his jacket and down the other side into his other pocket.

   Phil Drabble   *A weasel in my meatsafe*, 1977

The house-weasel managed to last for a long time after the introduction of the cat . . . In a play by Plautus (254–184 B.C.) a weasel, not a cat, catches a mouse at the feet of one of the actors.

   Edward Hyams   *Animals in the service of man*, 1972

Animals in the field

Bull

Bulls, that walk the pastures in kingly-flashing coats.
  George Meredith   *Phoebus with Admetus*, 1880

ANGRY BULL

An angry wild-bull, as swift as a horse, and fiercer than fifty
wild-cats, is a very terrible creature.
  John Masefield   *Lost endeavour*, 1910

From almost every farm a dreadful tale
Of what a bull had done made children quail . . .
How the bull, loose in meadow, chased and tossed
A little boy, who lived (with reason lost).
How one, pursued across a field, was torn:
'The bull had tatters of him on his horn'.
  John Masefield   *Going to see the bull*, 1942

Jack slipped down the tree and took to his heels.
Unfortunately the bull saw him; he immediately set up
another roar, and bounded after Jack. Jack perceived his
danger, and fear gave him wings; he not only flew across the
orchard but he also flew over the hedge, which was about five
feet high, just as the bull drove his head into it.
  Captain F. Marryat   *Mr Midshipman Easy*, 1836

I was cornered one day by a large and very uncertain-
tempered bull . . . The roof was too low for him to toss me so
he charged instead. Luckily the cowman was resourceful and
quick in action; he opened the gate against which I was
leaning, I fell out, the bull hesitated a moment, and the
cowman slammed the gate in his face.
  Mary Brancker   *All creatures great and small*, 1972

There is something peculiarly grim and hostile about the expression of a bull, with its thick neck and small roving eye, and one can never feel at ease in the presence of that mixture of fierceness and stupidity. If it has a ring in its nose, as many bulls have, that makes it all the worse.

The Times anthology, 1933

As I stepped forward with my ring the young bull and I stood face to face, and for a moment the wide-set eyes under the stubby horns looked into mine. As I reached out he must have moved slightly because the sharp end of the ring pricked him a little on the muzzle; the merest touch, but he seemed to take it as a personal insult because his mouth opened in an exasperated bawl and again he reared on his hind legs.

James Herriot   *Vet in harness*, 1974

John Small, who saved his life by playing his violin to a ferocious bull, to 'the admiration and perfect satisfaction of the mischievous beast', lived to be 89.

Eric Parker   *Highways and byways in Surrey*, 1908
[Small was a notable eighteenth-century cricketer.]

I saw the bull coming after me. He had come after me before but he had never caught me. I tried to get through the gate, but the bull caught me and struck me down. He had me down on the ground punishing me for half an hour . . . When I came to myself and stumbled into the house I was bruised all over and covered with blood.

Francis Kilvert   *Diary*, 1872

I have been told that a bull in the company of cows is not dangerous, but I know now that this is an old wives' tale. This bull had plenty of cows to keep him company, but it was my company he sought. I got myself over a tall thorn fence only at the very last moment.

Brian Vesey–Fitzgerald   *The Hampshire Avon*, 1950

'Tis pleasure to approach
And by the strong fence shielded, view secure
Thy terrors, Nature, in the savage bull.

James Hurdis   *The village curate and other poems*,
1788

How agreeable to watch, from the other side of the high stile, this mighty creature, this fat bull of Bashan, snorting, champing, pawing the earth, lashing the tail, breathing defiance at heaven and me . . . his heart hot with hate, unable to climb a stile.

   Rose Macaulay   *Personal pleasures*, 1935

When you take a bull by the horns . . . what happens is a toss-up.

   W. Pett Ridge   *Love at Paddington*, 1912

BULL SUBDUED

'I was stalkin' a lot of larks on me hands and knees, when a herd o' cattle come latherin' round me. So I makes a run at 'em on me hands and knees, and off they goes. All 'cept one. He was an owd bull. He stood and groaned. So, thinks I, if I can make the cows run I can make the master too. I hulls up a lot of grass and lets out a terrible row and makes a run at the guv'nor on me hands and knees. Blast! he went off like a train!'

   J. Wentworth-Day   *Farming adventure*, 1943
   [An old countryman is describing a boyhood incident.]

Why dost thou, bull and boar, so sillily
Dissemble weakness, and by one man's stroke die,
Whose whole kind you might swallow and feed upon?

   John Donne   *Holy sonnets*, 1633

See an old unhappy bull,
Sick in soul and body both,
Slouching in the undergrowth
Of the forest beautiful,
Banished from the herd he led,
Bulls and cows a thousand head.

   Ralph Hodgson   *The bull*, 1917

There are a couple of young pedigree bulls on the farm at the moment . . . When people describe terrorists or hooligans as behaving 'like animals' I think of the dignity and composure of the two little bulls and wonder what they mean.

   James Gladstone   in *Sunday Telegraph*, 16 Jan. 1984

BULL-BAITING

After dinner, with my wife and Mercer to the Beare-garden, where I have not been, I think, of many years, and saw some good sport of the bull's tossing of the dogs: one into the very boxes. But it is a very rude and nasty pleasure.

Samuel Pepys   *Diary*, 1666

I went with some friends to the Bear Garden, where was cock-fighting, bull and bear baiting . . . One of the bulls tossed a dog full into a lady's lap as she sat in a box at a considerable height from the arena. Two poor dogs were killed . . . and I most heartily weary of the rude and dirty pastime.

John Evelyn   *Diary*, 1670

Bull-baiting in any shape is irresistible to the Spaniard.

Richard Ford   *Handbook for travellers in Spain*, 1845

It is, I think, only a Spaniard who can really enjoy a bull-fight, which appeals with such irresistible force to all that is evil in him. Beneath the glaring sun, and with the blood of dying bullocks and tortured horses staining the sand of the arena, he finds himself in his proper element.

Stuart Cumberland   *A thought-reader's thoughts*, 1888

The formal bullfight is a tragedy, not a sport, and the bull is certain to be killed.

Ernest Hemingway   *Death in the afternoon*, 1932
[If not killed in the ring, the animal was slaughtered outside.]

Camel

SON OF THE DESERT

Our camels sniff the evening and are glad.

J. Elroy Flecker   *Hassan*, 1922

The Red Sahara . . . across its hollows trailed
Long strings of camels, gloomy-eyed and slow.

Jean Ingelow   *Poems*, 1885

Early in the morning the Syrian pilgrimage passed in
procession through the town. The important people rode in a
kind of closed litter carried by two camels, one before and the
other behind, and forming a very commodious conveyance.
The camels' heads were decorated with feathers, tassels, and
bells.

John Burckhardt   *Travels in Arabia*, 1830
[A Swiss traveller of the very early nineteenth century.]

A camel never journeys without his amulet. The commonest
protection is a string of coarse blue-glass beads hung on his
neck, and a little bag containing words from the Koran.

F. T. Elworthy   *The evil eye*, 1895

Patient of thirst and toil,
Son of the desert, even the camel feels
Shot through his withered heart, the fiery blast.

James Thomson   *The seasons*, 1727

It is a curious fact that camels walk more quickly and
straighter to the sound of singing.

Rosita Forbes   *The secret of the Sahara*, 1921

Camels should, if possible, be watered every day. They
cannot be trained to do without water, and though they can
retain one and a half gallons of water in the cells of the
stomach, four or five days' abstinence is as much as they can
stand.

C. J. Cornish   *Animals of to-day*, 1898

CAMELS IN DISTRESS

I made the discovery that the camelmen had commenced
opening veins in the camels' necks, and were drinking the
blood obtained thereby.

Donald G. Cameron   *A Saharan venture*, 1928

Kittens are treated to houses well heated,
And pigs are protected by pens;
But a camel comes handy wherever its sandy,
ANYWHERE does for me!

C. E. Carryl   *The song of the camel*, 1892

If a kneeling camel be only approached, and a stone as large
as a walnut laid on its back, it begins to remonstrate, groaning
as if it were being crushed to the earth by its load.

J. G. Wood   *Bible animals*, 1869

CURIOUS BEASTS

Camels are curious beasts, but we liked their curious ways. It
is very pleasant to dig one's bare toes into the soft curve of a
camel's neck, and to dig them in harder, and with jerks, in
order to make him trot.

William Donkin and Norman Pearn   *The Times
anthology*, 1933

When I dismounted I felt I never wanted to ride a camel
again. Having ridden 120 miles in five days I was too sore to
sit and too tired to stand.

C. W. Hill   *The spook and the commandant*, 1975

Many of us have been bitten by his long front teeth, trampled
over by his noiseless feet, deafened by his angry roar, and
insulted by the protrusion of his contemptuous upper lip. No
one who thus knows him at home retains a spark of belief in
the beast's patience, amiability, fidelity, or any other virtue.

Frances B. Cobbe   *False beasts and true*, 1876

But the commissariat cam-u-el, when all is said an' done,
'E's a devil an' a ostrich an' a orphan-child in one.

Rudyard Kipling   *Oonts*, 1892

Camels are surely the most superior of all created beings.
Furthermore they know it. Their look of scorn on passing
men has to be seen to be felt.

Lucie Street   *The tent pegs of heaven*, 1967

In Syria, once . . . a camel took charge of my overcoat while the tents were being pitched, and examined it with a critical eye all over, with as much interest as if he had an idea of getting one made like it; and then, after he had done figuring on it as an article of apparel, he began to contemplate it as an article of diet.

Mark Twain *Roughing it*, 1872

Camels have been photographed standing behind their owners and, with apparent ecstasy, inhaling the smoke from a hookah or hubble-bubble pipe.

Maurice Burton *Just like an animal*, 1978

The camel of the North [Mongolia] which can endure not only thirst but freezing cold, long spells of hunger, and a bed of snow, is not only the stronger but the better equipped species. By September it grows a garment of fur almost as thick as a buffalo robe, and equally cold-resisting.

C. J. Cornish *Animals of to-day*, 1898

CAMEL AND HORSE

Cyrus collected together all the camels which had come in the train of his army to carry provisions, and mounted riders upon them . . . The horse has a natural dread of the camel, and cannot abide either the sight or the smell of that animal. The two armies then joined battle, and immediately, the Lydian war-horses, seeing and smelling the camels, turned round and galloped away.

Herodotus *History* (abbreviated)
[Cyrus the Persian defeated Croesus of Lydia 546 BC]

Cow

Upavon is a nice clean village with a very pleasant smell of cows.

Brian Vesey–Fitzgerald *The Hampshire Avon*, 1950

'Cows are my passion. What I have ever sighed for, has been to retreat to a Swiss farm, and live entirely surrounded by cows – and china.' (Mrs Skewton)

Charles Dickens *Dombey and son*, 1848
[Mrs Skewton is an eccentric elderly lady.]

Mark Twain & the Camel.

Nowhere can I think so happily as in a train . . . I see a cow, and I wonder what it is like to be a cow, and I wonder whether the cow wonders what it is like to be me.

A. A. Milne   *If I may*, 1920

Mr John Coombs, a Wiltshire farmer, bald for twenty years, found hairs sprouting again after one of his cows licked the top of his head.

Sunday Telegraph, 4 March 1984

MILKING TIME

My cow gazed round at me mildly, chewing its cud, and, seeing my head conveniently against its flank, added to its comfort by leaning on me. I became aware that my head was no longer supported against the cow, but the cow was supported against my head.

Adrian Bell   *Corduroy*, 1930
[A first attempt at milking.]

All the good ideas I ever had came to me while I was milking a cow.

Grant Wood (American artist)   quoted in **Jonathan Green's** *Dictionary of contemporary quotations*, 1982

The cow is of the bovine ilk;
One end is moo, the other milk.

Ogden Nash   *The cow*

God's jolly cafeteria
With four legs and a tail.

E. M. Root   *The cow*

A cow should be milked clean. Not a drop, if it can be avoided, should be left in the udder.

William Cobbett   *Cottage economy*, 1822

A friendly tripod forms their humble seat,
With pails bright scour'd, and delicately sweet.
The full-charg'd udder yields its willing streams,
While Mary sings some lover's am'rous dreams.

Robert Bloomfield   *The farmer's boy*, 1800

I milked the cows with a great love for them, and found that I had only to milk a cow myself for its yield to go up.

Barbara Woodhouse *Talking to animals*, 1954

At first the natives declared that all their cows were unmarried; but our courier swore such a grand sonorous oath, and fingered the hilt of his sword with such a persuasive touch, that the land soon flowed with milk.

A. W. Kinglake *Eothen*, 1844
[The natives were inhabitants of a Balkan village.]

Stories of exhausted landgirls [in the Second World War] were almost universal . . . My favourite was of a kindly cow, who, as the weary landgirl staggered in to milk her, said sympathetically: 'You just hang on, dearie, and I'll jump up and down!'

Jilly Cooper *Animals in war*, 1983

COWS IN THE MEADOW

The two happiest moments of my life at Bath Farm were the first time I was left to milk Bess on my own, and the first time she came across the pasture when I called her.

Rachel Knappett *A pullet on the midden*, 1946
[A young landgirl in the Second World War.]

Bess was a lovely little creature . . . She had a rich, honey-coloured hide . . . brown velvet eyes, a shiny black nose, and slim fine legs. She was one of the prettiest animals I have ever seen.

Rachel Knappett *A pullet on the midden*, 1946

Straight to the meadow then he whistling goes;
With well-known halloo calls his lazy cows:
Down the rich pasture heedlessly they graze,
Or hear the summons with an idle gaze.

Robert Bloomfield *The farmer's boy*, 1800

Though she wore a loud bell, the cow had made the discovery that if she stood perfectly still it would not ring. So Sylvia had to hunt for her [in the bushes] until she found her.

Sarah Orne Jewett *A white heron*, 1886

They paused for a moment to look over the valley . . . Cow bells rose very faintly, like single drops of music distilled into this upper silence.

Margaret Kennedy *The constant nymph*, 1924

The lowing herd wind slowly o'er the lea.

Thomas Gray *Elegy in a country churchyard*, 1751

Here are the Highland cattle, with their long-haired ruddy coats, their bison heads, bold wild eyes peering out through the overhanging locks, and horns with a menacing up-lift and terribly keen at the points.

Phil Robinson *The poets' beasts*, 1885

Half the time they munched the grass, and all the time they lay
Down in the water-meadows, the lazy month of May.

James Reeves *Cows*, 1952

CHEWING THE CUD

Placid and habitual
As Yogi in their meditations, they perform
Their calm, slow, patient ritual . . .
They munch and ruminate their jaws
In a sidelong, automatic motion.

Clive Sansom *Cows*, 1962

The gum-chewing student,
The cud-chewing cow,
Are somewhat alike,
Yet different somehow.
Just what is the difference
I think I know now –
It's the thoughtful look
On the face of the cow.

Anon. in John Davies, *Everyman's book of nonsense*, 1981

I always feel at home in a cow byre . . . I like to stand in front of a cow and look into her rather staring eyes, laugh at the sideways waggle of her jaws, and wait for the inevitable hiccup after turnips which is part of the mealtime ritual in cowland.

David Thurston Smith *Thistledown*, 1933

COW AND CALF

He saw a calf that had just been born on the steep slope of a field. As he stopped to look, the new-born calf began to slide helplessly down the grassy hill. The mother cow gave a strange cry and at once six other cows ran and stood in a line on the hill and stopped the calf sliding any further.

Maurice Burton *Just like an animal*, 1978

She was licking her gawky black calf
Collapsed wet-fresh from the womb, blinking his eyes
In the low morning dazzling washed sun.
Black, wet as a collie from a river, as she licked him,
Finding his smells.

Ted Hughes *Birth of a rainbow*, 1979

I heard of late of a cow in Warwickshire which in six years had sixteen calves, that is, four at once in three calvings and twice twins, which unto many may seem a thing incredible.

William Harrison *Elizabethan England*, 1577

I met my match with a mad cow. She had come to me a few days before calving, and had then seemed a nice quiet creature. Unfortunately she calved in the field, and when I tried to get her in she went mad . . . She just lowered her head and came at me at a pace which Spanish bullfighters would have welcomed.

Barbara Woodhouse *Talking to animals*, 1954

The cares created by the cow are amply compensated for by the education that these cares will give to the children . . . They will learn to set a just value upon dumb animals, and will grow up in the habit of treating them with gentleness . . . It may be the best way to sell the calf as soon as calved; if you cannot sell it, knock it on the head as soon as calved.

William Cobbett *Cottage economy*, 1822
[Cobbett's view of gentleness may be thought a trifle eccentric.]

COW ANECDOTES

I decided I would break in one of the heifers, to be ridden. The light roan one was my choice, and I found her extremely amenable . . . I rode her all round the roads just like a pony.

Barbara Woodhouse *Talking to animals*, 1954

The cows were brought over [from Alderney] in the Channel cutters, the other cargo usually consisting of cider. One boat was thirteen days out, and the captain, running short of water, tapped the cider casks. The cows enjoyed it so much that for three days they would drink nothing else.

C. J. Cornish *Animals of to-day*, 1898

An old lady had an Alderney cow, which she looked on as a daughter. Great was the sympathy and regret when, in an unguarded moment, the poor cow tumbled into a lime-pit. The poor beast lost most of her hair and came out looking naked, cold, and miserable . . . Captain Brown advised: 'Get her a flannel waistcoat and flannel drawers, ma'am.' By-and-by all the town turned out to see the Alderney meekly going to her pasture, clad in dark grey flannel.

Mrs E. C. Gaskell *Cranford*, 1853

An early seventeenth century diarist recorded how 'four drunken fellows' in Derbyshire drove a recently calved cow into church, 'and that which is appointed for churching a woman they read for the cow, and led her about the font: a wicked and horrible fact'.

Keith Thomas *Religion and the decline of magic*, 1971
[To 'church a woman' is to read the appointed service when a woman comes to church after a confinement.]

A cow is a very good animal in the field, but we turn her out of a garden.

Samuel Johnson in Boswell's *Life of Johnson*, 1791

In the close electrical kind of heat that precedes a thunderstorm . . . the cows give warning by scampering about in the wildest and most ludicrous manner – their tails held up in the air – tormented by insects.

Richard Jefferies *Wild life in a southern county*, 1879

A farmer in Toronto is hoping to make money by renting out space on the side of his cows . . . He is offering a three-foot-by-two-foot piece of oil-cloth strapped to a cow's side with an advertising message prominently displayed.

Daily Telegraph, 28 March 1984

Cattle are very scared with the smell or sight of blood . . . As soon as they put their noses down to where the blood is on the ground, they put their tails up and gallop away, bellowing, at a terrible rate.

Captain F. Marryat *The children of the New Forest*, 1847

COW HATER

You are not beautiful; you are far from clean; and the melancholy cries with which you rend the evening skies are like steamers that take the ocean, or sirens in a fog.

Rose Macaulay *Personal pleasures*, 1933

COW AND ARTIST

Eshley had conceived and executed a dainty picture of two reposeful milch-cows in a setting of walnut tree and meadow-grass . . . As he had begun, so, of necessity, he went on. His *Noontide Peace*, a study of two dun cows under a walnut tree, was followed by *A Mid-day Sanctuary*, a study of a walnut tree with two dun cows under it.

'Saki' *The stalled ox*, 1914

When a cow came slouching by in the field next to me, a mere artist might have drawn it; but I always get wrong in the hind legs of quadrupeds. So I drew the soul of the cow . . . all purple and silver.

G. K. Chesterton *A piece of chalk*, 1909

I never saw a purple cow,
I never hope to see one;
But I can tell you, anyhow,
I'd rather see than be one.

F. Gelett Burgess *The purple cow*, 1895

COWS CAUSING CONSTERNATION

Though generally placid, cows can be, if they choose, both obstinate and wild.

  Esther Meynell *Cottage tale*

There was an old man who said, 'How
Shall I flee from this horrible cow?
I will sit on this stile, and continue to smile,
Which may soften the heart of that cow.'

  Edward Lear *The book of nonsense*, 1846

A tender, timid maid! who knew not how
To pass a pig-sty, or to face a cow.

  George Crabbe *The widow's tale*, 1817–18

Coleridge came in . . . with a branch of Mountain Ash. He had been attacked by a cow.

  Dorothy Wordsworth *Journal*, 1802

A little after two o'clock the people in the Royal Exchange were much alarmed by the appearance of a cow, hard driven for Smithfield . . . and great confusion ensued, some losing hats and wigs, and some their shoes, while others lay about the ground in heaps.

  The Annual Register, January 1761

On October 8, 1871, a disastrous fire burned out an area in Chicago of more than three square miles, destroyed more than 17,000 buildings, left 100,000 people homeless, and cost 250 lives. According to legend, the fire was caused by a Mrs O'Leary's cow, who is said to have kicked over a lantern in the barn.

  Charles Neider *Man against nature*, 1955

In North Wales it was reported in 1589 that people still crossed themselves when they left their cattle . . . If any misfortune befell them or their animals the common saying was 'You have not made the sign of the cross upon the cattle'.

  Keith Thomas *Religion and the decline of magic*, 1971

Donkey

Methought I was enamour'd of an ass.

William Shakespeare *A midsummer night's dream*,
1595

'Janet! Donkeys!'
   Janet came running up the stairs . . . darted out on a little
piece of green in front, and warned off two saddle-donkeys
that had presumed to set foot on it.

Charles Dickens *David Copperfield*, 1849–50
[Janet's mistress, Miss Trotwood, strongly objected to
donkey-boys who allowed their animals to tread on a patch
of grass in front of her garden.]

DONKEY DETERMINATION

The ass thinks one thing, and he that rides him another.

Thomas D'Urfey *Comical history of Don Quixote*,
1694

Blucher could do nothing at all with his donkey . . . The road
was fenced in with high stone walls, and the donkey gave him
a polishing, first on one side and then on the other. He finally
came to the house he (the donkey) was born in, and darted
into the parlour, scraping Blucher off at the doorway.

Mark Twain *The innocents abroad*, 1869

I proceeded to steer Modestine through the village. She tried,
as was indeed her invariable habit, to enter every house and
every courtyard in the whole length.

R. L. Stevenson *Travels with a donkey*, 1879

Better strive with an ill ass than carry the wood one's self.

Thomas Fuller *Gnomologia*, 1732

Your dull ass will not mend his pace with beating.

William Shakespeare *Hamlet*, 1603

AN OPPRESSED RACE

One of our over-loaded donkeys collapsed while descending a
pass . . . Its driver, in true Oriental fashion, tried to pull it up
by the tail, causing the poor moke a certain amount of pain. I

waxed very wroth with the driver, whom I regret to say I
knocked down. He apologised humbly for not pulling the tail
harder!

T. Howard Somervell   *After Everest*, 1936

And when that donkey looked me in the face
His face was sad.

James and Horace Smith   *Playhouse musings*, 1812

Poor little foal of an oppressed race!
I love the languid patience of thy face:
And oft with gentle hand I give thee bread,
And clap thy ragged coat, and pat thy head . . .
Or is thy sad heart thrilled with filial pain
To see thy wretched mother's shortened chain?
And truly, very piteous is *her* lot –
Chained to a log within a narrow spot
Where the close-eaten grass is scarcely seen.

S. T. Coleridge   *To a young ass, its mother being
tethered near it*, 1794

BIZARRE OR BEWITCHING?

With monstrous head and sickening cry
And ears like errant wings,
The devil's walking parody
On all four-footed things.

G. K. Chesterton   *The donkey*, 1900
[A libel on the donkey's charming appearance, if not on its
voice.]

She looked smaller than ever standing there in the lane, with
her shaggy brown coat, ears like a toy rabbit, and a set of
sturdy little long-furred legs . . . The Rector's wife went into
ecstasies over her.

Doreen Tovey   *Donkey work*, 1962

Men came down with donkeys almost invisible beneath light
loads of furze. The sweet faces of the donkeys peeped out
bewitchingly from under their loads: they looked perfectly
happy. (Afghanistan)

Lucie Street   *The tent pegs of heaven*, 1967

FAMILY FRIEND

What a wonderful family friend to have, loyal, uncriticizing
(except perhaps when you are late with breakfast), and with
such beautiful long ears into which to pour your troubles,
safe in the knowledge that no gossip will be carried to the
neighbours.

Monica Sternberg   *My wishes were donkeys*, 1972

The donkeys and the men, women, and children all eat and
sleep in the same room, and are unclean, ravaged by vermin,
and truly happy.

Mark Twain   *The innocents abroad*, 1869

Nicholas Nye was lean and grey,
Lame of leg and old,
More than a score of donkey's years
He had seen since he was foaled.

Walter de la Mare   *Nicholas Nye*, 1913

I have seen strange dogs threatened seriously by donkeys and
put to flight, and I have been told by old shepherds that a
donkey is a great protection for sheep, watching over the
flocks . . . and braying loudly when danger threatens.

Monica Sternberg   *My wishes were donkeys*, 1972

His mistress ran a one-woman hire service with a donkey and
cart. To advertise her services she had taken part in a
carnival, dressing up the donkey's legs in two pairs of her
open-legged calico drawers, with frills round the bottoms.

Winifred Foley   *A child in the forest*, 1977

Goat

There is no house possessing a goat but a blessing abideth
therein.

Mohammedan saying

The dingy kidling, with its tinkling bell,
Leaped frolicsome, or old romantic goat
Sat, his white beard slow waving.

S. T. Coleridge   *Sibylline leaves*, 1817

Lying there, I heard the gentle, drowsy tinkling of a goat-bell, and presently the herds wandered past us, pausing to stare with vacant yellow eyes, bleat sneeringly, and then move on.

   Gerald Durrell   *My family and other animals*, 1956

A dirty and smelly nanny goat is invariably the victim of dirty and insanitary living quarters and of an owner who is too lazy to groom her.

   David Le Roi   *Goats*, 1978

When the 5th Canadian Infantry Battalion were sent to the Front [in First World War] they were told that Sergeant Billy, their goat mascot, must be left behind in Canada. This caused an uproar. 'We can get another colonel,' said the soldiers unanimously, 'but not another goat!'

   Jilly Cooper   *Animals in war*, 1983

GOAT'S MILK

Not even the pig has so varied a diet as the goat. It consumes and converts into milk great quantities of garden stuff. It enjoys the prunings and loppings of bushes and trees . . . all the hedge-trimmings, even those of the thorn fences.

   C. J. Cornish   *Animals of today*, 1898

Goats will eat mouldy bread or biscuit; fusty hay and almost rotten straw; furze bushes, heath thistles, and, indeed, what will they not eat, when they will make a hearty meal on paper, brown or white, printed on or not printed on, and give milk all the while!

   William Cobbett   *Cottage economy*, 1822

By the side of Loch Ness I perceived a little hut . . . Mr Fraser allows an old man and his wife to live in this hut, and keep sixty goats. They lived all the Spring upon milk and curds and whey alone.

   James Boswell   *Journal of a tour to the Hebrides*, 1785

I find among the writers that the milk of the goat is next in estimation to that of the woman, for that it helpeth the stomach.

   William Harrison   *Elizabethan England*, 1577

GOATS AND GULLIBILITY

Plutarch says that the women of Crete, seeing how the goats, by eating the herb dittany, caused arrows to fall from their wounds, learnt to make use of the plant to aid them in childbirth.

Phil Robinson   *The poets' beasts*, 1885

The goat was honoured as the representation of manhood in its most complete vigour, and was even worshipped from gratitude to the gods, for causing the people of that country [Egypt] to multiply.

William J. Fielding   *Strange superstitions*, 1945

In Italy and Spain the Devil himself, in the shape of a goat, used to transport witches on his back, which lengthened or shortened according to the number of witches.

Charles Mackay   *Extraordinary popular delusions*, 1841

Formerly the Devil himself was depicted as a goat, and the animal is also a type of lust and lechery.

William Rose Benet   *The reader's encyclopedia*, 1948

GOATISH INTELLIGENCE

The name 'goat' has become . . . almost synonymous with 'brainless' and 'silly'. But to associate 'goat' with 'silliness' is manifestly unjust, as anyone who has kept a goat well knows. So far from being silly, the goat is a highly intelligent animal.

David Le Roi   *Goats*, 1978

The smile of the Goat has a meaning that few
Will mistake, and explains in a measure
The Censor attending a risqué Revue
And combining Stern Duty with pleasure.

Oliver Herford   *The smile of the goat*, 1912

All goats are mischievous thieves, gate-crashers, and trespassers. Also they possess individual character, intelligence, and capacity for affection which can only be matched by the dog. Having once become acquainted with them I would as soon farm without a dog as without a goat.

David Mackenzie   *Farmer in the Western Isles*, 1954

BACK TO THE WILD

One day
Its rope of twisted straw
Snapped, and it passed away
Forever from the circle of man's law,
Up to the tameless hills to be untamed as they.

   John Redwood Anderson   *The goat*

The high hills are a refuge for the wild goats.

   Book of Common Prayer, Psalms, 1552

Horse

A horse! a horse! my kingdom for a horse!

   William Shakespeare   *Richard III,* 1597

He doth nothing but talk of his horse.

   William Shakespeare   *The Merchant of Venice,* 1600

LOVE OF HORSES

God forbid that I should go to any heaven in which there are
no horses.

   R. B. Cunninghame Graham   *Letters*

A horse misused upon the road
Calls to Heaven for human blood.

   William Blake   *Auguries of innocence, c.* 1801

People may talk of first love – it is a very agreeable event, I
daresay – but give me the flush, and triumph, and glorious
sweat of a first ride.

   George Borrow   *Lavengro,* 1851

She would wait at village inns for hours, finally, when she
judged my stay long enough, tapping at the snuggery window
with her nose.

   James Agate   *Ego 2,* 1936

There is no secret so close as that between a rider and his
horse.

   R. S. Surtees   *Mr Sponge's sporting tour,* 1853

When I breathe down my nose to say how do you do to a horse, it can hear that breath at anything up to twenty yards, for horses have the most acute sense of hearing.

Barbara Woodhouse   *Talking to animals*, 1954

She loved the horses. Every day at the same hour she would drive down to see them – and above all she loved The Prince. He would prick up his ears when he heard the wheels on the gravel.

A. Conan Doyle   *The adventure of Shoscombe Old Place*, 1927

A pony is always companionable and often a helpmate. Tim, for instance, made friends as soon as he arrived here. Each morning he came to meet me at the fence, shaking his nostrils rather as men shake hands.

J. H. B. Peel   *Latest country talk*, 1981

We attended stables, as we attended church, in our best clothes, thereby no doubt showing the degree of respect due to horses.

Osbert Sitwell   *The scarlet tree*, 1945

The horse that carried Miss Kilmansegg
Was a very rich bay called Banker . . .
And then when Banker obtained a pat,
To see how he arched his neck at that!
He snorted with pride and pleasure!

Thomas Hood   *Miss Kilmansegg and her precious leg*, 1841

FLIES AND TAILS

Three cart-horses were looking over a gate
Drowsily through their forelocks, swishing their tails
Against a fly, a solitary fly.

Edward Thomas   *The manor farm*, 1914

Horses, resigned to their black plague of flies,
Peer over hedges, where ditch-water dries . . .
But for a silken rustle of oats, or swish
Of a slow tail, the tyranny of Noon
Is absolute.

Geoffrey Johnson   *Drought*, 1948

I never knew the *flies* so troublesome in England as I found them on this ride [North Hampshire]. I was obliged to carry a great bough, and to keep it in constant motion, in order to make the horse peaceable enough to enable me to keep on his back.

   William Cobbett   *Rural rides*, 1830

The tail is the horse's natural protection against flies. It is also an aid in taking a corner. The horse will turn at top speed, using his tail as a rudder.

   Daily Mail, 9 May 1913

He stirs not head not hoof although
The grass is fresh beneath the branch;
His tail alone swings to and fro
In graceful curves from haunch to haunch.

   William Canton   *Day-dreams*, 1896

HORSE AND HARROW

Only a man harrowing clods
In a slow silent walk
With an old horse that stumbles and nods
Half asleep as they stalk.

   Thomas Hardy   *In time of 'The Breaking of Nations'*, 1916

Had Hardy ever done any harrowing . . . he would have found, as I found, that, despite appearances, one's mind is kept fully occupied seeing that none of the work is missed, that one does not overturn the harrows, that none of them is clogged or caught up in another. Stumble, yes; but that has nothing to do with drowsiness.

   Adrian Bell   *Corduroy*, 1930

HORSE-LANGUAGE

The ploughmen chatter continuously to the pairs of horses which pull their ploughs. Many of the competitors have had to borrow both ploughs and horses locally . . . The strange beasts respond perfectly to the ploughmen's horse-language, which to urban ears is as meaningless as a dog's bark.

   The Times anthology, 1933

Albert used to say, 'Talk or whistle all the time while following a young horse [i.e. carriage-driving] and it will never go wrong' . . . for while the horse knew you were there its ears twitched back and forth in confidence.

Fred Kitchen *Brother to the ox*, 1942

Don't go cluck-cluck with your tongue and teeth. This is strictly taboo, don't ask me why, unless you are driving a horse in harness, or lungeing, or moving him over in the stable.

Monica Dickens *Talking of horses . . .*, 1973

HORSE MAGIC

On the arrival of foals . . . it was the custom to call in the assistance of an aged man of wisdom . . . In some mysterious way his simple presence and goodwill – gained by plentiful liquor – was supposed to be efficacious against accident and loss.

Richard Jefferies *Wild life in a southern county*, 1879

A white witch practised her craft [in West Kent] until twenty years ago . . . She once demonstrated her power over animals by placing a piece of straw in the road in front of a horse, and in spite of every persuasion the animal obstinately refused to move.

Eric Maple *The dark world of witches*, 1962

In Britain horse magic was often practised on farms in pre-tractor days. Men who claimed to have complete power over any horse, however difficult, were known as the Brotherhood. There was reputed to be a secret word which the 'horse-whisperers' (as the Brotherhood were sometimes called) murmured into a horse's ear.

Geoffrey Lamb *Magic, witchcraft, and the occult*, 1977

The smith uttered a word I had never heard before, in a sharp, pungent tone. The horse forthwith became like one mad, and reared and kicked with the utmost desperation . . . He uttered another word in a voice singularly modified, but sweet and almost plaintive. The animal lost all its fury, and became at once calm and gentle.

George Borrow *Lavengro*, 1851

WHITE HORSE AND WHITE LEG

White horses were counted in my childhood, and a train journey was enlivened by watching from the windows for a white horse grazing in a field. Each horse brought luck to the viewer.

  Alison Uttley *The button-box*, 1968

A pathetic sight at the funeral of King George V was His Majesty's favourite pony, Jock, saddled . . . The pony beautifully groomed, his milk-white coat a dazzling contrast to the prevailing black, was led by a groom from the Sandringham stables.

  Illustrated London News, 1 Feb. 1936

One white foot – buy him;
Two white feet – try him;
Three white feet – look well about him;
Four white feet – go without him!

  Old English rhyme

The old superstition is that if a horse has one white leg you should certainly keep it for yourself. If it has two, then give the animal to a friend. If it has three or four, then it is no good.

  Charles Platt *Popular superstitions*, 1925
  ['White leg' refers to the area around the hoof.]

The mare stood kicking slightly with a white hind foot and whisking her tail. Her bright coat shone in the sunlight, and little shivers and wrinklings passed up and down its satin because of the flies.

  John Galsworthy *Had a horse*, 1923

NOBLE STEEDS

'Bring forth the horse!' – the horse was brought;
In truth he was a noble steed,
A Tartar of the Ukraine breed,
Who look'd as though the speed of thought
Were in his limbs.

  Lord Byron *Mazeppa*, 1819

His mane is like a river flowing,
And his eyes like embers glowing
In the darkness of the night,
And his pace as swift as light.

Barry Cornwall *The blood horse*, 1822

He bounds from the earth as if his entrails were hairs. When I
bestride him, I soar, I am a hawk; he trots the air; the earth
sings when he touches it. (The Dauphin)

William Shakespeare *Henry V*, 1599

If your horse be nimble, and apt thereto by nature, you may
make him a Stirer, by teaching him to bound aloft.

Thomas Blundeville *The fower chiefyst offices*,
1565–6

Anyone who knows and understands horses appreciates that
if you frighten a horse at a fence he will not go near that fence
again. The essential thing is to make a horse enjoy his
jumping.

Harvey Smith *V is for victory*, 1972

DANGEROUS MOMENTS

The narrow track traversed the face of cliffs so sharp that we
had to haul at the bridles and grip the tails of the ponies to
prevent them rolling sheer down into the torrent below.
(Greece)

H. W. Nevinson *Changes and chances*, 1923

Often the track was cut out of a perpendicular mountain wall
. . . One day Gato stepped too near the edge, and some loose
rocks gave way under his hind leg. He lost his footing and
shot over the side and went sliding towards the edge of a deep
precipice.

A. F. Tschiffely *Tschiffely's ride*, 1952
[The horse was saved by a tree, and later rescued.]

I felt confident that the hardy ponies used in Northern China
and Manchuria would be useful [in Antarctica] . . . They are
accustomed to handling heavy loads in very low
temperatures, and they are hardy, sure-footed, and plucky.

Ernest Shackleton *The heart of the Antarctic*, 1909

One day in 1733, when out hunting, Paulet St John came suddenly upon a chalk-pit. Too late to avoid it, he let his gallant horse take the leap over a terrible drop of 25 feet. The daring steed leaped safely over.

Arthur Mee *The king's England: Hampshire*, 1939
[A monument marks the place where the leap took place, on Farley Down, near Winchester.]

AT THE GALLOP

Imagine the mail [coaches] assembled on parade in Lombard Street . . . Then come the horses. Horses! Can these be horses that bound off with the actions and gestures of leopards? What stir! – What a thundering of wheels! – What a trampling of hoofs!

Thomas De Quincey *The English mail coach*, 1849

I sprang to the stirrup, and Joris, and he;
I galloped, Dirck galloped, we galloped all three . . .
Behind shut the postern, the lights sank to rest,
And into the midnight we galloped abreast.

Robert Browning *How they brought the good news from Ghent to Aix*, 1842

Under his spurning feet the road
Like an arrowy Alpine river flowed,
And the landscape sped away behind
Like an ocean flying before the wind,
And the steed, like a barque fed with furnace ire,
Swept on, with his wild eyes full of fire.

T. Buchanan Read *Sheridan's ride*, 1865

Oh, for a good fat horse or two to carry me Westward Ho –
To carry me Westward Ho, my boys, that's where the cattle stray
On the far Barcoo, where they eat nardoo, a thousand miles away.

Australian bush song
[Barcoo – river in S. Australia; nardoo – clover-fern.]

He flung himself on his horse and rode off madly in all directions.

Stephen Leacock *Nonsense novels*, 1911

A handsome foal with a bell about his neck came charging up
to us upon a stretch of common, sniffed the air martially as
one about to do great deeds; and suddenly thinking otherwise
in his green young heart, put about and galloped off as he had
come.

R. L. Stevenson   *Travels with a donkey*, 1879

Broad-backed they gallop, the mares who have not foaled,
Out of the blue-grey distance heavy with sleep;
They trample the grasses, tousled and frosted deep,
Their eyes flame back the diamonds of the cold.

Geoffrey Johnson   *The mares*, 1946

HOSTILE HORSES

We were taught to restrain horses by picking up one front
foot. This in theory meant that it was impossible for the
animal to use one of the remaining three legs for kicking.
Unfortunately some horses are able to defy the laws of gravity
and can remain upright on two legs while they deliver a
powerful and well-aimed blow with the third.

Mary Brancker   *All creatures great and small*, 1972
[A veterinary surgeon's experiences.]

I was offered a ride on a horse by a customer, dared not
refuse, and was tossed up on to a terrifying mountain of
herculean muscle which heaved under me like the sea. 'I want
to get off!' I screamed.

Emlyn Williams   *George*, 1961
[A childhood memory.]

A horse is dangerous at both ends and uncomfortable in the
middle.

Ian Fleming   quoted in *Sunday Times*, 9 Oct. 1966

Anyone who is concerned about his dignity would be well
advised to keep away from horses.

Duke of Edinburgh   *Men, machines and sacred
cows*, 1984

There are two important rules in horse-riding. The first is to
mount the horse. The second is to stay mounted.

Anon.

The more Mr Winkle tried to get nearer him, the more he
sidled away; and notwithstanding all kinds of coaxing and
wheedling, there were Mr Winkle and the horse going round
and round each other for ten minutes, at the end of which
time each was precisely the same distance from the other as
when they commenced.

Charles Dickens *The Pickwick papers*, 1837–9

His horse coming slap on its knees with him, threw
Him head over heels, and away it flew.

R. H. Barham *The smuggler's leap*, 1842

The line of beauty to a horse is a curve rather than a straight
line, as can be gathered from the pleasurable look on horses'
faces as they watch the arc of trajectory taken by their riders
over high hedges at a hunt meet.

John Harrold *How to be happy with a horse*, 1963

A horse which stops dead just before a jump and thus propels
its rider into a graceful arc provides a splendid excuse for
general merriment. It has happened to me.

Duke of Edinburgh *Men, machines, and sacred
cows*, 1984

A hedge ahead . . . Cantilever sprang at it. Next moment her
head seemed miles below me and I was flying through the air
. . . I hit the ground with my shoulder, then stood on my
head. I seemed poised thus for ages. It felt undignified; I kept
wishing my legs would come down.

Adrian Bell *Corduroy*, 1930

Oh wasn't it naughty of Smudges?
Oh, Mummy, I'm sick with disgust.
She threw me in front of the judges,
And my silly old collarbone's bust.

John Betjeman *Hunter trials*, 1954

I began to kick, and plunge, and rear as I had never done
before . . . For a long time he stuck to the saddle and
punished me cruelly with his whip and spurs; but my blood
was thoroughly up, and I cared for nothing he could do if

only I could get him off. At last, after a terrible struggle, I threw him off backwards. I heard him fall heavily upon the turf, and galloped off.

Anna Sewell   *Black Beauty*, 1877
[Ginger, a chestnut mare, is talking to Black Beauty.]

SELLING A HORSE

Let a woman be as false as she can . . . she is, compared with the man who wishes to sell you a horse, openness and truth itself.

W. H. Hudson   *The purple land*, 1885

The ways of a man with a maid be strange, yet simple and tame
To the ways of a man with a horse, when selling or racing the same.

Rudyard Kipling   *Certain maxims of Hafiz*, 1886

HORSE-RACING

The impressions received from the St Leger race-week were not favourable. It was noise and turmoil all day long, and a gathering of vagabonds from all parts of the racing earth. Every bad face that had ever caught wickedness from an innocent horse had its representative in the Doncaster streets.

John Forster   *Life of Charles Dickens*, 1872–4

Everyone knows that horse-racing is carried on mainly for the delight and profit of fools, ruffians, and thieves.

George Gissing   *The private papers of Henry Ryecroft*, 1903

I saw a string of racehorses being led past. My father said, 'Just look at those useless animals of Beaverbrook's'. But I sat there completely transfixed. I'd never known there was such beauty.

David Swannell   quoted in *Telegraph Sunday Magazine*, 3 March 1983
[Swannell, later the Jockey Club's senior handicapper, had been taken to Newmarket when he was nine years old.]

The stable-boys thud by
Their horses slinging divots at the sky
And with bright hooves
Printing the sodden turf with lucky grooves.

Andrew Young *Wiltshire Downs*, 1950

Except by accident, the race-horse never trots. He must
either walk or gallop; and in exercise, even when it is the
hardest, the gallop begins slowly and gradually, and increases
till the horse is nearly at full speed.

Thomas Holcroft *Memoirs*, 1816

The field came in sight up the hill, the crowd yelled and
struggled . . . The horses thundered down to the Corner; she
had to stand on tiptoe to see them, and then she could see
only a flying muddle of colour. They went too fast.

A. P. Herbert *The water gipsies*, 1930

'Sir Robert has got to win this Derby. He's up to the neck,
and it's his last chance. Everything he could raise or borrow is
on the horse.'

A. Conan Doyle *The adventure of Shoscombe Old
Place*, 1927

Alas! it is the painful fact
That horses hardly ever act
As anyone expected.

A. P. Herbert *The racing-man*, 1931

The first favourite was never heard of, the second favourite
was never seen after the distance post, all the ten-to-oners
were in the rear, and a dark horse which had never been
thought of . . . rushed past the grandstand in sweeping
triumph.

Benjamin Disraeli *The young duke*, 1831

Lord Hippo suffered fearful loss
By putting money on a horse
Which he believed, if it were pressed,
Would run far faster than the rest.

Hilaire Belloc *More peers*, 1911

In 1669 Charles II began his regular pilgrimages to
Newmarket, making it his spiritual home and horse-racing
the sport of kings.

Christopher Falkus *The life and times of Charles II,*
1972

Crowds that from Newmarket spread,
And o'er the heath confus'dly tread . . .
List to the word impetuously
'They're off, they're off', now here, now gone,
And quick the vigorous race is run.

Kenrick Prescot *To the counsellor,* 1722

Horse-racing would not be the exciting diversion it is unless
the horses were, as they are, bred for the purpose – were, in
fact, professionals. A match between a couple of dray horses
would have little interest – except, perhaps for the horses
themselves.

Illustrated Sporting and Dramatic News, 18 Oct. 1890

Mule

Smokin' my pipe on the mountings, sniffin' the mornin' cool,
I walks in my old brown gaiters along o' my old brown mule.

Rudyard Kipling *Screw-guns,* 1892

They came to a rise, steeper than the last. 'Hand on mane!'
cried Martin. Gerard obeyed, and the mule helped him up
the hill faster even than he was running before.

Charles Reade *The cloister and the hearth,* 1861

I was riding a mule that had very tender feet . . . when it came
near to a place where it could escape the deep mud by going
over a stony part, it would slacken its pace and look first at
the mud, then at the stones, evidently balancing in its mind
which was the lesser evil.

Thomas Belt *Naturalist in Nicaragua,* 1874

A stick is something to which no Mexican mule ever pays the
slightest attention.

Aldous Huxley *Beyond the Mexique Bay,* 1934

The man was a zealous member of the Greek Church. He had been a tailor . . . Every now and then his mule, forgetting that its rider was a saint and remembering that he was a tailor, took a quiet roll upon the ground.

 A. W. Kinglake *Eothen*, 1844

The load is lashed to the yokes with leather thongs, and it needs two men to take it off. When this was done the mule retreated a step or two and bowed his head as though he were bowing his thanks for the release.

 W. Somerset Maugham *The gentleman in the parlour*, 1930

Hambone, a pack mule attached to the United States army . . . could stand flat-footed and jump a five-foot fence without touching it.

 Eric Delderfield *Second book of true animal stories*, 1972

A frosty morning! We must take care not to touch metal. A mule made his way into my tent and looked for something edible in my washing-basin. To his great astonishment it stuck to his nose.

 Sven Hedin *To the forbidden land*, 1934

I once saw a mule with legs so striped that anyone at first would have thought it must have been the product of a zebra.

 Charles Darwin *On the origin of species*, 1859

Ox

He stands like an ox in the furrow.

 Rudyard Kipling *Norman and Saxon*, 1911

The strong laborious ox, of honest front,
Which incomposed he shakes; and from his sides
The troublous insects lashes with his tail.

 James Thomson *The seasons, summer*, 1727

Drooping, the labourer-ox
Stands cover'd o'er with snow, and then demands
The fruit of all his toil.

 James Thomson *The seasons, winter*, 1726

Oxen could thrive on forage that horses would not touch.
Often they kept going on cottonwood twigs and leaves when
no grass was available.

Edwin Way Teale *Autumn across America*, 1956

It does one's heart good to see the thirsty oxen rush into a
pool of delicious rain-water. In they dash until the water is
deep enough, and then they stand drawing slowly in the long
refreshing mouthfuls, until their formerly collapsed sides
distend as if they would burst.

David Livingstone *Travels in South Africa*, 1858

The oxen of this country [Cape of Good Hope] are large and
wonderfully fat and tame. Upon the fattest among them the
Negroes place a pack saddle made of reeds, and upon this
saddle they place a kind of litter made of sticks, upon which
they ride.

First voyage of Vasco da Gama, 1497–9

He who drives fat oxen should himself be fat.

Samuel Johnson in Boswell's *Life of Johnson*, 1791
[Johnson is parodying a line in Henry Brooke's *Earl of
Essex*, 1778]

When the oxen be very young, many graziers will oftentimes
anoint their budding horns with honey, which mollifies the
natural hardness of that substance, and thereby maketh them
to grow unto a notable greatness.

William Harrison *Elizabethan England*, 1577

Why should I pause, poor beast, to praise
Thy back so red, thy sides so white;
And on thy brow those curls in which
Thy mournful eyes take no delight.

W. H. Davies *Collected poems*, 1923

While leanest beast in Pastures feed,
The fattest ox the first must bleed.

Robert Herrick *Hesperides*, 1648

He who to wrath the ox has mov'd
Shall never be by woman lov'd.

William Blake *Auguries of innocence, c.* 1801

Going to church in a village not far from Lewes, I saw an ancient lady of very good quality drawn to church in her coach with six oxen: nor was it done but out of mere necessity, the way being so stiff and deep that no horses could go in it.

  Arthur Young   *Tour through the southern counties*, 1768

A bad omen seems to be drawn from an ox or cow breaking into a garden. Some cattle were driven close to my house, and the back gate being open three got into our little bit of garden. When our drudge came in the afternoon, she said it was a bad sign, and that we should hear of three deaths within the next six months.

  L. S. in *Notes and queries*, 1859

'There is an ox in my garden,' Adela announced . . .
'How did it get into the garden?' asked Eshley.
'I imagine it came in by the gate,' said the lady impatiently;
'it couldn't have climbed the walls, and I don't suppose anyone dropped it from an aeroplane as a Bovril advertisement. The immediately important question is not how it got in but how to get it out.'

  'Saki' *The stalled ox*, 1914

Pig

He took me down to see the pigs . . . and we talked pigs all the way.

  A. A. Milne *Mr Pim passes by*, 1922

FLOWERS AND FOOD

The gardeners had told the Prince that you couldn't have pigs and flowers, so he decided to have pigs.

  'Saki' *The story-teller*, 1914

The hog by chance one morning roamed . . .
For food the garden then he scours,
Treading down painted ranks of flowers,
Upturning them as, left and right,
He delves to quench his appetite.

  John Gay *Fables*, 1727 (modernized)

Her ringed snout still keeps her to the sty.
Then out he lets her run; away she snorts
In bundling gallop for the cottage door.

Edmund Blunden   *Poor man's pig*, 1922

Pigs organize trespassing parties, which grow bolder daily.
One day they come round and look at the back door. The next
day one runs into the passage and pokes his nose into the
kitchen.

C. J. Cornish   *Animals today*, 1898

A herd of bristly swine is pricked along;
The filthy beasts, that never chew the cud,
still grunt, and squeak, and sing their troublous song,
And oft they plunge themselves the mire among.

James Thomson   *The castle of indolence*, 1748

One of the common barnyard sows,
Mire-smirched, blowzy,
Maunching thistle and knotweed on her snout-cruise –
Bloat tun of milk
On the move, hedged by a litter of feat-foot ninnies.

Sylvia Plath   *Sow*, 1957

From oak to oak they run with eager haste . . .
The trudging sow leads forth her numerous young,
Playful, white and clean, the briars among.

Robert Bloomfield   *The farmer's boy*, 1800

CLEAN AND CLEVER

In its natural state it is cleanly both in food and person, of
remarkable intelligence, activity, and courage.

Phil Robinson   *The poets' beasts*, 1885

The work of teaching and organizing the others fell naturally
upon the pigs, who were generally recognized as being the
cleverest of the animals.

George Orwell   *Animal farm*, 1945

A peculiarity of the Amazing Pig of Knowledge is that he
knew the value of money. He could also tell black from white,

distinguish colours, with a shrewd eye count his audience,
and even tell people their thoughts.

Henry Morley *Memoirs of Bartholomew Fair*, 1859

He takes it for granted, or grunted, that we understand his
language, and without servility or insolence he has a natural,
pleasant, hail-fellow-well-met air with us.

W. H. Hudson *The book of a naturalist*, 1919

There is nothing a pig loves more than a good bath, with a
loofah and plenty of soap flakes . . . There is something
delightfully lovable about a really clean pig, in clean yellow
straw.

Barbara Woodhouse *Talking to animals*, 1954

The sow moves on mincing feet
Across the field to a tree
Stump, lays her chin on the gold
Grain of wood and explores it
To cure her itch.

Patricia Beer *In the field*, 1975

This sow was grown very sagacious and artful; when she
found occasion to converse with a boar she used to open all
the intervening gates, and march by herself up to a distant
farm where one was kept.

Gilbert White *Natural history of Selborne*, 1776

PIG TALES

An acquaintance of my own, a successful pig-keeper, had a
sow so in love with him that while she would tolerate male
visitors accompanying her master to the sties, she would at
once attack any woman.

Edward Hyams *Animals in the service of man*, 1972

One disadvantage of being a hog is that at any moment some
bleeding fool may try to make a silk purse out of your wife's
ear.

J. B. Morton (Beachcomber) *By the way*, 1931

It is a curious fact that the pig, though naturally a timorous
animal, is yet moved to pugnacity if his brother is attacked.

Adrian Bell *Corduroy*, 1930

In the market-place of Macon, Comte [the famous French
ventriloquist and conjurer] inquired the price of a pig which a
peasant woman had for sale. He pronounced it extortionate.
'Piggy,' said Comte gravely, 'is the good woman asking a fair
price for you?' 'Too much by half,' the pig seemed to reply. 'I
am measled, and she knows it!'

Thomas Frost *Lives of the conjurers*, 1876

Hunting the Pig is a favourite rustic pastime. The tail of the
animal is well soaped . . . and he who can catch him with one
hand and hold him by the stump of the tail without touching
any other part, obtains him for his pains.

Joseph Strutt *Sports and pastimes*, 1801
[Sometimes, as the following quotation shows, the animal's
whole body was greased.]

Monstrous fun it makes to hunt the pig,
As soaped and larded through the crowd he flies;
Thus turn'd adrift he plays them many a rig . . .
And still his slippery hide all hold denies.

John Clare *The village minstrel*, 1819

The habit of tail-biting in pigs is probably as old as thumb
sucking in babies.

Mary Brancker *All creatures great and small*, 1972

Even a baby pig a few hours old is capable of putting up a
piercing squealing, audible half-a-mile away. This little
animal is the noisiest of all babies, and is almost always
squealing unless it is either glued to a teat or delightfully
asleep.

R. H. Smythe *How animals talk*, 1959

In a Hampshire village a cottage took fire one evening. A sow
with her young ones appeared on the scene and dashed into
the flames. The people rushed to the rescue, and with some
difficulty pulled the pigs out . . . This is a case of the hypnotic
effect of fire on [some] animals.

W. H. Hudson *Hampshire days*, 1903

In the Highlands . . . sailors and fishermen rarely mention
the animal by its proper name, but refer to it by some term of

their own . . . To meet a pig on the way to the boat is very
unlucky.

    Christina Hole   *English folklore*, 1940

Sheep

He's a great lover of animals . . . animals know. Even sheep
know. He can do anything he likes with them.

    Christopher Fry   *Boy with a cart*, 1939

His sheep his children are, each one he knows.

    Edmund Blunden   *Shepherd*, 1922

SHEEP IN THE FOLD

Far off, the pearly sheep
Along the upland steep
Follow their shepherd from the wattled fold,
With tinkling bell-notes falling sweet and cold.

    Rosamund Marriott Watson   *A summer night*, 1895

I never hear the sheep-bells in the fold . . .
Without a strong
Leaping of recognition; only here
Lies peace beyond uneasy truancy.

    V. Sackville-West   *The land*, 1927

'It's lonesome with the flock on the downs; more so in cold
wet weather, when perhaps you don't see a person all day.
The bells keep us from feeling it too much. They're company
to us.' (A shepherd)

    W. H. Hudson   *A shepherd's life*, 1910

Here will I sit and wait
While to my ear from uplands far away
The bleating of the folded flocks is borne.

    Matthew Arnold   *The scholar gipsy*, 1853

The sheepfold here
Pours out its fleecy tenants o'er the glebe.
At first, progressive as a stream, they seek
The middle field; but scatter'd by degrees,
Each to his choice, soon whiten all the land.

    William Cowper   *The task*, 1785

SHEEP MAY SAFELY GRAZE

Sheep grazed the field; some with soft bosom press'd
The herb as soft, while nibbling stray'd the rest.

William Cowper   *The needless alarm*, 1794

Not far away the woolly sheep moved about in their pen of
hurdles, some cropping the grass (the farmer could hear the
sound of tearing, and a muffled bleat now and then as they
moved about the fold).

'B.B.'   *Wild lone*, 1938

Sheep will eat what cattle will not and where they will not . . .
In fact, sheep should be kept on every farm. Not to compete
with cattle but to prevent waste.

Brian Vesey-Fitzgerald   *The Hampshire Avon*, 1950

SHEEP-WASHING

Sheep-washing was going on in the valley below . . . Four or
five young men, and one amazon of a barefooted girl, stood in
the water where it was pent between two hurdles, ducking,
sousing, and holding down by main force the poor,
frightened, struggling sheep, who kicked, and plunged, and
bleated, and butted, and would certainly have committed
half-a-dozen homicides if their power had equalled their
inclination.

M. R. Mitford   *Our village*, 1819

Early July is washing-time around Dyffrin . . . Many cars
stop when we are at work there, and excited visitors run
across with cameras. When one of them asks what is
happening, someone answers 'We be teaching them to swim!'

Thomas Firbank   *I bought a mountain*, 1940

They drive the troubled flocks, by many a dog
Compelled, to where the mazy-running brook
Forms a deep pool . . . And oft the swain,
On some impatient seizing, hurls them in.

James Thomson   *The seasons, summer*, 1727

They haul themselves ashore. With outraged cries
They waterfall uphill, spread out and stand
Dribbling salt water in flowers' eyes.

Norman MacCaig   *Sheep dipping*, 1965

SHEEP-SHEARING

Wool-buyers like the sheep to be shorn within ten days of washing. The short interval does not allow grease to accumulate again in the wool.

Thomas Firbank *I bought a mountain*, 1940

How meek, how patient, the mild creature lies!
Fear not, ye gentle tribes, 'tis not the knife
Of horrid slaughter that is o'er you waved;
No, 'tis the tender swain's well-guided shears.

James Thomson *The seasons, summer*, 1727

There are two feasts annually held among the farmers of this country. The first is sheap-shearing . . . celebrated in ancient times with feasting and a variety of rustic pastimes.

Joseph Strutt *Sports and pastimes*, 1801

We still have about four hundred Scottish Blackfaced sheep. We do not kill them but just use them for their wool and let them die naturally from old age . . . Paul has written a few songs about wild life, including a song about a baby lamb.

Linda McCartney (wife of former member of the Beatles) in *Animals* (RSPCA), autumn, 1979

Through its wool the sheep has had a major impact on the history of mankind.

M. L. Ryder *Sheep and man*, 1983

SHEEP IN TROUBLE

A 'casualty sheep' is one that has fallen lame or sick, and has had to be killed, or perhaps has been found dead.

Eric Parker *Surrey*, 1947

[The 'sick' ewe] eluded me effortlessly and shot past me with a thundering of hooves. I gave chase for twenty yards but it was too hot . . . In any case, I have long held the notion that if a vet can't catch his patient there's nothing much to worry about.

James Herriot *Vet in harness*, 1974

A sheep came plunging through the river, stumbled up the bank, and passed close to us. It had been frightened by a little insignificant dog on the other side.

Dorothy Wordsworth *Journal*, 1802

Look how a panicked flock will stare,
And huddle close and start and wheel about,
Watching the roaming mongrel here and there.

Thomas Hood **1845**

A gentleman relates that his shepherd one evening found the sheep in confusion, and upwards of twenty bitten, some of whom never recovered, and others brought dead lambs. A single dog, it was suspected, caused all the mischief.

Richard Jefferies *Field and farm*, 1883

The hunted fox was a great danger to sheep when the chase brought the animal near if not right into the flock. He [the shepherd] had one dreadful memory of a hunted fox trying to lose itself in his flock, and the hounds following it and driving the poor sheep mad with terror.

W. H. Hudson *A shepherd's life*, 1910

Sheep are such senseless creatures that they are liable to be stampeded by the veriest trifle.

Ernest Thompson Seton *Lobo*, 1900

Of course sheep sometimes panic when frightened; so do humans. Of course sheep will follow a leader; so will humans.

Brian Vesey-Fitzgerald *Animal anthology*, 1965

Flocks of sheep, sometimes left unattended . . . display constantly a great deal more awareness than groups of people, and are wide awake at all times and ready to respond to a signal which the modern human being would understand only after it had been carefully explained to him.

R. H. Smythe *How animals talk*, 1959

The bleating kind
Eye the bleak heavens, and next the glistening earth,
With looks of dumb despair, then sad dispers'd
Dig for the wither'd herb, through heaps of snow.

James Thomson *The seasons, winter*, 1726

The sheep feed stolidly, nor know
How near their heads the lightnings go.
  Nora Chesson *Sheep in a storm*, 1906

The sheep get up and make their many tracks,
And bear a load of snow upon their backs,
And gnaw the frozen turnip on the ground
With sharp quick bite.
  John Clare *Sheep in winter*, 1857

SHEEP SUPERSTITIONS

The Greeks thought that a garment made from the fleece of a
sheep that had been torn by a wolf hurt the wearer, setting up
an itch or irritation in his skin.
  James G. Frazer *The golden bough*, 1890–1915

In times of drought the Guanches of Teneriffe led their sheep
to sacred ground, and there they separated the lambs from
their dams, that their plaintive bleating might touch the heart
of the god (who would weep rain).
  James G. Frazer *The golden bough*, 1890–1915

YOUNG LAMBS

Lambs are calling upon the hill
With a bleating, wavering, quavering cry,
Calling and calling, they don't know why.
  Eiluned Lewis *Morning songs*, 1944

No matter how often you have done it, it is always a pleasure
successfully to assist an old ewe who is having difficulty, to
put the steaming soaking lamb in front of her and watch her
start to clean it up, to see it shake its ears loose for the first
time, and wobble up on its legs.
  James Gladstone in *Daily Telegraph*, 3 May 1983

Those that only roam the fields when they are pleasant in
May see the lambs at play in the meadow, and naturally think
of lambs and May flowers. But the lamb was born in the
adversity of snow.
  Richard Jefferies *The open air*, 1885

It was the time of year
Pale lambs leap with thick leggings on
Over small hills that are not there.
Andrew Young   *A prehistoric camp*

Did your eye brighten when young lambs at play
Leap'd o'er your path with animated pride,
Or gaz'd in merry clusters by your side?
Robert Bloomfield   *The farmer's boy*, 1800

Well pleased I view the rampant lambs unite
To race, or match themselves in mimic fight,
Or through the prickly furze adventurous roam
Till by their milky mothers summon'd home.
William Stewart Rose   *To Hookham Frere*, 1834

And then a little lamb bolts up behind
The hill and wags his tail to meet the yoe [ewe],
And then another, sheltered from the wind,
Lies all his length as dead – and lets me go
Close by, and never stirs.
John Clare   *Young lambs*, 1820

There is a party of these young lambs as wide-awake as heart
can desire; half-a-dozen of them playing together, frisking,
dancing, leaping, butting, and crying in the young voice,
which is so pretty a diminutive of the full-grown bleat.
M. R. Mitford   *Our village*, 1819

All the lamb family are as full of quaint fun as Charles
himself:
Colonel E. B. Hamley   *Our poor relations*, 1872

It is quite clear when lambs burst out laughing. They throw
their hind legs in the air, wiggle their catkin tails before
galloping off madly. Then they return to crush heads with
any other lamb available.
Elma M. Williams   *The Pant Glas story*, 1970

The early lambs, still
Fleecy, look bulkier now
Than their shorn mothers.
Patricia Beer   *January to December*, 1975

Little lamb, who made thee?
Dost thou know who made thee?
Gave thee life and bid thee feed
By the stream and o'er the mead:
Gave thee clothing of delight,
Softest clothing, woolly, bright;
Gave thee such a tender voice
Making all the vales rejoice?

   William Blake   *The lamb*, 1789

The Derby ram

As I was going to Derby
All on a market day
I met the finest ram, sir,
That ever was fed on hay.

This ram was fat behind, sir,
This ram was fat before,
This ram was ten yards round, sir,
Indeed he was no more.

The horns that grew on his head, sir,
They were so wondrous high
As I've been plainly told, sir,
They reached up to the sky.

   Anon.   *The Derby ram*

Animals in the wild

Ant bear (Anteater)

The ant bear isn't a bear at all, and he is one of Nature's
caricatures, with the body of a red pig, the hind legs of a
kangaroo, and the ears of a donkey.

June Kay   *The thirteenth moon*, 1970

Normally the ant-bear is a harmless creature, but although it
has no teeth it is a dangerous animal to provoke, for its
forelegs and claws are lethal offensive and defensive weapons.
If it can manage to embrace its opponent with its forelegs, the
unfortunate victim has little chance of escaping.

David Attenborough   *Zoo quest to Guiana*, 1956

Sarah Huggersack [was] a baby giant anteater who had to be
bottle-fed, and whose idea of ecstasy was to cling, with razor-
like claws, either to Gerry or to me, or better still, to a straw-
filled sack. Gerry simply adored her and she him . . . She
shared his bed at night ('she mustn't catch cold') and his
every free moment.

Jacquie Durrell   *Beasts in my bed*, 1967

Antelope

The wild antelope, that starts whene'er
The dry leaf rustles in the brake

P. B. Shelley   *Alastor*, 1815

The little duiker let me stroke her warm body while she
waggled a stumpy tail. But she would not allow me to touch
her black velvet muzzle, which was soft as shammy-leather.

Elspeth Huxley   *The flame trees of Thika*, 1959

Mr David Attenborough & Ant-eater.

It is contrary to all the basic instincts of survival for a wild antelope to be confined at night, for when confronted with danger, its first defence is in being able to run and outpace an enemy.

Daphne Sheldrick   *My four-footed family*, 1979

The antelope has a long slit beneath each eye, which can be opened and shut at pleasure. On holding an orange to one, the creature made as much use of these orifices as of his nostrils, applying them to the fruit, and seeming to smell it through them.

Thomas Pennant   *Letter to Gilbert White*, 1768

The topi is a fairly mad animal, a large brown gleaming antelope with gun-metal blazes on its legs and an air of continual stage-fright.

Alan Moorehead   *No room in the ark*, 1959

Ape

There are one hundred and ninety-three living species of monkeys and apes. One hundred and ninety-two of them are covered with hair.

Desmond Morris   *The naked ape*, 1967
[The odd one out is, of course, man.]

These pieces of moral prose have been written by a large carnivorous Mammal, belonging to the sub-order of the Animal Kingdom which includes also the Orang-outang . . . and the gentle Chimpanzee.

Logan Pearsall Smith   *All trivia*, 1934

The ugliest ape that ever was born is all the more repellent for being so like a man.

Robert Lynd   *The book of this and that*, 1915

Baboons and apes ridiculous we find,
For what? For ill resembling human kind.

William Congreve   *Works of Mr Congreve*, 1710

Though he endeavour all he can
An ape will never be a man

George Wither   *Emblems*, 1635

Apes are apes though clothed in scarlet.

Ben Jonson   *The poetaster*, 1601

Men laugh at apes; they men condemn,
For what are we but apes to them?

John Gay   *Fables*, 1727

Man is distinguished from the man-like apes by the greater
relative size of his brain and the portion of the skull in which
it is contained.

Richard Lydekker   in *Harmsworth natural history*,
1910

There are two kinds of monsters common to the woods of
Angola (West Africa); the largest of them is called *pongo*
(gorilla) in their language . . . They have no understanding
beyond instinct. When the people of the country travel
through the woods they make fires in the night, and in the
morning the *pongos* will come and sit round it till it goes out,
for they do not possess sagacity enough to put on more wood.

Andrew Battel   in **Samuel Purchas**, *Purchas his
pilgrimage*, 1612

Presently before us stood an immense male gorilla . . . He
stood there, and beat his breasts with his huge fists till it
resounded like an immense bass-drum, which is their mode
of offering defiance, meanwhile giving vent to roar after roar.

Paul du Chaillu   *Explorations in equatorial Africa*,
1861

On being alarmed the orang-utan retreated towards the
jungle, and a number of men ran out to intercept him. The
man who was in front tried to run his spear through the
animal's body, but the mias [orang] grasped it in his hands,
and in an instant got hold of the man's arm, which he seized
in his mouth, making the teeth meet in the flesh above the
elbow.

Alfred Russell Wallace   *The Malay archipelago*, 1869
[More sympathy must go to the defensive ape, which was
later killed, than to the aggressive man.]

In a fight the chimpanzee kills the leopard occasionally by
seizing both paws and biting them, so as to disable them.

David Livingstone   *Last journals*, 1874

I saw one female chimpanzee, newly arrived in a group, hurry up to a big male and hold her hand towards him. Almost regally he reached out, clasped her hand in his, drew it towards him, and kissed it with his lips.

Jane Van-Lawick Goodall *In the shadow of man,* 1971

Badger

Brocks snuffle from their holt within
A writhen root of blackthorn old . . .
They stretch and snort and sniff the air,
Then sit to plan the night's affair.

Eden Phillpotts *The badgers*

Here in the furze is the haunt of the badger . . . He may be traced in the rabbit 'buries', where he enlarges a hole for his habitation, sleeps during the day, and comes forth in the gloaming. In summer he digs up the wasps' nests, not, as has been supposed, for the honey, but for the white larvae they contain.

Richard Jefferies *The gamekeeper at home,* 1878

The badger in this part of the country is rather a vagrant, moving about from wood to wood . . . A badger or two in a large wood, where rabbits are plentiful, will do very little harm, and it seems absurd to levy war on these interesting creatures.

George A. B. Dewar *Wild life in Hampshire highlands,* 1899

The badger is a quiet, inoffensive, peace-loving animal. Terrible when roused, and potentially the most formidable beast we have in England, he does not attack unless forced to do so.

W. Kay Robinson *Britain's beasts of prey,* 1949

The senseless and cruel practice of badger-baiting, now illegal but still followed in some places, is but a reflection of man's inhumanity.

Alfred Leutscher in *Animals* (RSPCA), autumn, 1979

They get a forked stick to bear him down,
And clap the dogs and take him to the town,
And bait him all the day with many dogs.

John Clare   *The badger*, 1835

A badger never soils its home. Instead, small pits are dug
nearby and used as toilets.

Alfred Leutscher   in *Animals* (RSPCA), autumn,
1979

They always spring-clean their nests – throw out the old
bedding and bring in new – before their cubs are born.

Percy Edwards   *Percy Edwards' country book*, 1980

There are many myths about the badger; one of the most
popular being badger funerals, in which a ritual is said to be
observed while burying the dead. In fact, badgers dispose of
their dead by walling them up underground – presumably for
reasons of hygiene.

Ernest Neal   in *Telegraph Sunday Magazine*, 5 Aug.
1984

His strength and patience quite amazed me. One morning I
found the heavy long-handled hydraulic jack in the garage
fully extended. Fifteen up and down strokes are needed to
lever it to this position, so either he had operated it at
intervals during the night, or had tackled it at one go, like one
possessed.

Jane Ratcliffe   *Fly high, run free*, 1979

Bat

Twinkle, twinkle, little bat!
How I wonder what you're at!
Up above the world you fly!
Like a teatray in the sky.

Lewis Carroll   *Alice's adventures in wonderland*,
1865

When Vesper trails her gown of grey
Across the lawn at six or seven
The diligent observer may
(Or may not) see, athwart the heaven,
An aimless rodent on the wing. Well that
Is (probably) a Bat.

  A. A. Milne   *The day's play*, 1910

Now air is hush'd, save where the weak-ey'd bat
With short shrill shriek flits by on leathern wing.

  William Collins   *Ode to evening*, 1747

Bats, and an uneasy creeping in one's scalp
As the bats swoop overhead!
Flying madly.

  D. H. Lawrence   *Bat*, 1923

There is a very general belief that if a bat alights on a
woman's head, it becomes entangled in her hair and cannot
get away . . . [In 1959] three gallant young women allowed
the Earl of Cranbrook to thrust a bat into their hair . . . In
each case the creature escaped quite easily.

  Christina Hole   *Encyclopedia of superstitions
  (revised)*, 1961

I was much entertained last summer with a tame bat, which
would take flies out of a person's hand. If you gave it
anything to eat, it brought its wings round before the mouth,
hovering and hiding its head.

  Gilbert White   *Natural history of Selborne*, 1767

The bat was not only tame but showed intelligence enough to
recognize its master and fly to him. Immediately the man
entered the room the bat recognized and welcomed him with
its cries, and if not at once taken up to be petted, climbed up
his dress, rubbed its head against him, and licked his hands.

  Ernest A. Bryant   in *Harmsworth natural history*,
  1910

Strange revelation! Warm as milk,
Clean as a flower, smooth as silk!
O what a piteous face appears,
What great fine thin translucent ears!

  Ruth Pitter   *The bat*, 1950

With zig-zag wing a flitter-mouse
Flew in and out the haunted house.

　Eden Phillpotts　*The ghost*, 1922

Bear

BROWN BEAR AND GRIZZLY

In the night, imagining some fear,
How easy is a bush suppos'd a bear!

　William Shakespeare　*A midsummer night's dream*,
　c. 1595

She will sing the savageness out of a bear.

　William Shakespeare　*Othello*, 1604

When the Himalayan peasant meets the he-bear in his pride,
He shouts to scare the monster, who will often turn aside.

　Rudyard Kipling　*The female of the species*, 1921

In the Himalayas, at least, the brown bear never attacks
human beings if unmolested.

　Richard Lydekker　*The brown bear*, 1910

Never drop your gun to hug a bear.

　H. E. Palmer　*A fable*, 1946

This is the chase: I am gone for ever.
(*Exit Antigonus, pursued by a bear.*)

　William Shakespeare　*The winter's tale*, c. 1609

The grizzly bear is huge and wild;
He has devoured the infant child.
The infant child is not aware
He has been eaten by the bear.

　A. E. Housman　*Infant innocence*, 1936

Isn't it funny
How a bear likes honey?
Buzz! Buzz! Buzz!
I wonder why he does.

　A. A. Milne　*Winnie-the-Pooh*, 1926

He who shareth honey with the bear hath the least part of it.

Thomas Fuller *Gnomologia*, 1732

BENEVOLENT BRUIN

Folklore, as a rule, is just; and folklore is always kind to the bear. There are no fairy-tales or legends in which the bear is a villain. He is a blundering fool in several fables, but he is never unamiable.

Phil Robinson *The poets' beasts*, 1885

'Who's been sleeping in *my* bed?' said Father Bear in his great big voice.

The three bears (folk tale)
[The familiar Goldilocks story has been nicely reversed in the following quotation.]

One evening I returned to the cabin to find that a bear had broken in, turned the place upside down, and gone to sleep in mother's bed.

Evelyn Bergland (woman trapper) quoted in *Everybody's Weekly*, 1936

There was an old person of Ware
Who rode on the back of a bear.

Edward Lear *Book of nonsense*, 1846

In Siberia a mother one day missed her two children, one aged six, the other four. She went to the forest to look for them, and there, to her horror, she saw them close to a great wild bear. When she recovered from the first shock she found that one of them was feeding the creature with strawberries, and the other was actually riding on its back.

J. G. Wood *Glimpses into petland*, 1863

A common belief was that if a child rode on a bear's back he would never catch whooping-cough in the future, and if he already had it, he would be cured.

E. & M. A. Radford *Encyclopedia of superstitions*, 1948

HIBERNATION

By mid-October . . . the black bear has his hibernaculum [place of hibernation] selected, and will go in when snow comes. He does not like the look of his big tracks in the snow. They publish his goings and comings too plainly.

John Burroughs *Autumn tides*, 1893

While they are extremely fat at the beginning of their winter sleep, they are reduced to little more than skin and bone at its close.

Richard Lydekker *The brown bear*, 1910

POLAR BEAR

The white bears all in a dim blue world
Mumbling their meals by twilight.

Jean Ingelow *Poems*, 1885

Slow o'er the printed snows with silent walk
Huge shaggy forms across the twilight stalk.

Erasmus Darwin *Poetical works*, 1806

Polar bears rarely hurry. They appear to pause and consider. If they are perplexed, they yawn. If they have nothing else to do they take a snooze, often lying with their head resting on one incurved paw.

Richard Davids *Lords of the Arctic*, 1983

Dr Kane well observes that there is something grand in this tawny savage [polar bear], never leaving this utter destitution, this frigid inhospitableness; coupling in May and bringing forth its young at Christmas – a gestation carried on entirely below zero, and more than half of it in Arctic darkness – living in perpetual snow. This Polar animal has no time for hibernation; his life is one long winter.

Arctic voyages and discovery, 1860

We discovered this morning the damage done [by a polar bear] to a cask of oil. It was of strong oak staves, well secured by thick, broad hoops of birch. Yet with one blow of his tremendous paw he had snapped off the four hoops and broken the staves short.

George Cartwright *Journals*
[Major Cartwright explored Labrador in the late seventeenth century.]

Beaver

The tail of this beast is like unto a thin whetstone, as the body unto a monstrous rat: the beast also itself is of such force in the teeth that it will gnaw a hole through a thick plank in a night.

William Harrison *Elizabethan England*, 1577

Their strength is amazing. They cut down trees forty feet high with their huge, chisel-like teeth, roll and float them into position for their dams, then dig up boulders from the streambed to pile on top.

Marjorie Sykes in *Animals* (RSPCA), autumn, 1979

Around A.D. 1600 about sixty to a hundred million beavers lived there [North America]; they were hunted but at the same time protected and revered by their friends the Indians, who believed that Manitou, the Great Spirit, first created the beaver and then man. Many Indian tribes thought they were descendants of the 'Great Beaver'.

Bernhard Grzimek *Wild animal, white man*, 1966

The beaver is not a fisherman; but at times he interferes sadly with those who must follow that craft for a living. When he builds his dam on a trout stream it means an end of fishing in that neighbourhood. The trout cannot stand his commotions.

William J. Long *Woodfolk comedies*, 1920

Boar

This foul, grim, urchin-snouted boar.

William Shakespeare *Venus and Adonis*, 1593

He slew
That cruel boare, whose tusks turn'd up whole fields of grain,
And rooting, raised hills upon the level plaine.

Michael Drayton *Polyolbion*, 1622

His snout digs sepulchres where'er he goes;
Being mov'd, he strikes whate'er is in his way,
And whom he strikes his cruel tushes slay.

William Shakespeare *Venus and Adonis*, 1593

General Howe turned out some German wild boars and sows
in his forests, to the great terror of the neighbourhood . . . but
the country rose upon them and destroyed them.

Gilbert White *Natural history of Selborne*, 1789

To fly the boar before the boar pursues
Were to incense the boar to follow us,
And make pursuit where he did mean no chase.

William Shakespeare *Richard III*, 1597

Have ye seen the tusky boar . . .
On surrounding foes advance?

Thomas Gray *The death of Hoel*, 1768

The jungles of South America are full of large herds of wild
pigs, which, in bulk, are the most dangerous animals in the
wild. They are quite fearless, and by reason of their numbers
can pull down anything in their path.

Julian Duguid *Green hell*, 1931

When they are in herds they can be fairly easily located . . . as
the noise they make when feeding is considerable, but a lone
pig will lift his snout to listen and sniff the air intently every
few minutes . . . After his first fright the pig usually stops,
and there is a loud blowing noise as he clears his nostrils the
better to catch the scent. (Malaya)

F. Spencer Chapman *The jungle is neutral*, 1949

Wild pig breed in the same kind of jungle [as elephant], and
harbour their sucking pigs under huge heaps of leaves and
grass which in size and appearance resemble ant-heaps four
feet high.

J. H. Williams *Elephant Bill*, 1950

Buffalo

Oh give me a home where the buffalo roam!
  Brewster Higley   *Home on the range*, 1873

The American bison in its native country is almost invariably
misnamed the buffalo.
  Harmsworth natural history, 1910

The mad
Masterful tramping of the bison herds
Tearing down headlong, with their bloodshot eyes
In savage rifts of hair.
  Jean Ingelow   *Poems*, 1885

The American buffalo has become almost extinct. A few
scattered herds still survive among the foothills and parks of
the Rocky Mountains, but ceaseless, senseless slaughter has
at last reduced the once innumerable herds of buffaloes to a
straggling handful.
  Achilles Daunt   *The three trappers*, 1882

William Cody's killing of buffalo was no more exceptional
than that of all the other [cowboys] with whom the great
plains swarmed in an era when thirty-one million of these
distracted creatures were ruthlessly slaughtered for their
hides, or for the amusement of wealthy American and English
sportsmen.
  Times Literary Supplement, 1929
  [William Cody was the famous Buffalo Bill.]

Here was a young buffalo, a splendid beast from the
southernmost plains of the Lower Niger . . . His bulging eyes
looked at me in stupefaction. He snorted and bellowed,
stamped, and pawed a hole in the ground. Never before had a
white man crossed his view.
  Andre Demaison   *The new Noah's ark*, 1941

The bison, fiercest race of Scotland's breed,
Whose bounding course outstripped the red deer's speed,
By hunters chased, encircled on the plain,
He, fuming, shook his yellow lion-mane,
Spurned with black hoof, in bursting rage, the ground,
And fiercely tossed his moony horns around.
  John Leyden   *Scottish descriptive poems*, 1802

But he, though irked by noise and stir, is loth
To leave the wallowing-pool that coats his sides
And back and belly with protective ooze
  Herbert Price *The buffalo*, 1914
  [The buffalo is 'teased all day by clouds of stinging flies'.]

Water buffaloes are said to learn tricks easily; one is reported
to have learned to fetch water from a river with a bucket
carried on one of its horns.
  Osmond P. Breland *Animal friends and foes*, 1958

It is well-known that the buffalo herd is a close social group
and that individuals get protection from each other. When
you approach a herd they will first run together and then turn
round and face you, all heads pointing towards you.
  Ernest Neal *Uganda quest*, 1971

Presently I came face to face with a buffalo standing stock
still in the middle of the road . . . Since his horns were
enormous and his eyes far from friendly I thought it prudent
to make a slight detour.
  W. Somerset Maugham *The gentleman in the
parlour*, 1930

The herd came bounding past us. We took refuge on an old
ant-hill, and I had a good opportunity of seeing that the
leader was an old cow; all the others allowed her a full half-
length in their front. On her withers sat about twenty
buffalo-birds . . . When the buffalo is quietly feeding, this
bird may be seen sitting on its back ridding it of the insects
with which their skins are sometimes infested.
  David Livingstone *Travels in South Africa*, 1857

Cheetah

When he [Kublai Khan] rides about his enclosed forest he
has one or more small leopards [cheetahs] carried on
horseback behind their keepers; and when he pleases to give
directions for their being slipped, they instantly seize a stag,
or a goat, or a fallow deer.
  Marco Polo *Travels*, dictated 1298

The very head of the animal is small, and combines to assist its speed. No animal on earth can travel for five hundred yards, or perhaps a little more, so fast as the cheetah. Its legs are long and made for speed.

F. G. Alexander in *Harmsworth natural history*, 1910

The great spotted cat is the fastest thing alive. When some years ago cheetahs were raced against greyhounds in England, the cheetahs jumped clean over the greyhounds' backs to get to the front.

Alan Moorehead *No room in the ark*, 1959

Coyote

Blown out of the prairie in twilight and dew,
Half bold and half timid, yet lazy all through;
Loth ever to leave, and yet fearful to stay,
He limps in the clearing – an outcast in grey.

F. Bret Harte *Coyote, c.* 1869

The coyote is so spiritless and cowardly that even while his exposed teeth are pretending a threat, the rest of his face is apologising for it.

Mark Twain *Roughing it*, 1872

The young man of the house had shot a little wolf called a coyote in the early morning. The heroic little animal lay on the ground, with his big furry ears, and his clean white teeth . . . but his brave little life was gone . . . risking his life so cheerfully – and losing it – just to see if he could pick up a meal near the hotel.

William James *Letters*, 1920

Deer

THE FAWN'S LIGHT FEET

The young fawns are playing with the shadows.

Elizabeth Barrett Browning *The cry of the children*, 1850

The bounding fawn, that darts across the glade
When one pursues, through mere delight of heart.

  William Cowper   *The winter walk at noon*, 1785

Tremendous excitement ensues when we first glimpse the
little Bambis, so small, no larger than hares, but with long
spindly legs and beautifully mottled coats.

  Jane Ratcliffe   *Fly high, run free*, 1979

I can hear again, after all the years, the patter of the fawn's
light feet, I can see the dark eyes of the young creature
trotting up to me as I sat among the chestnut trees. And then
the wind changed, perhaps, or I moved, and the fawn knew
its danger and leapt away from me.

  Eric Parker   *Surrey*, 1947

Fawns are extremely difficult things to handle when they
become frightened; their hind legs must be held . . . I took off
my shirt and wrapped her in it, so that even if she did
struggle she could not injure herself or us.

  Gerald Durrell   *The drunken forest*, 1961

For it was full of sport, and light
Of heart, and did invite
Me to its game: it seemed to bless
Itself in me; how could I less
Than love it? O, I cannot be
Unkind to a beast that loveth me.

  Andrew Marvell   *The nymph complaining for the
death of her fawn*, 1681

I have seen a hind trying to defend her calf from an eagle,
rearing up with her ears back and slashing viciously with her
fore-hooves each time he stooped with an audible rush of
wind . . . Though she never touched more than a wingtip the
eagle grew wary and finally sailed off down the glen.

  Gavin Maxwell   *Ring of bright water*, 1960

Out in the dark over the snow
The fallow fawns invisible go
With the fallow doe.

  Edward Thomas   *Out in the dark*, 1918

FOREST AND PARK

In the Holt Forest, where a full stock of fallow-deer has been kept up till lately, no sheep are admitted. The reason, I presume, being that sheep are such close grazers, they would pick out all the finest grasses, and hinder the deer from thriving.

Gilbert White *Natural history of Selborne*, 1789

Endless herds of deer, of all varieties of colours; and what adds greatly to your pleasure in such a case, you see comfortable retreats prepared for them in different parts of the woods [Petworth Park, Sussex].

William Cobbett *Rural rides*, 1830

As on occasion I was unable to draw stags from memory I hastened to Richmond Park, where there are whole herds of them. They come up close to people without the least fuss, and they show a preference for vegetarians.

Karel Capek *Letters from England*, 1925

A great deal of well-intentioned harm is done to tame deer in parks and zoos. They are often fed tit-bits by adoring children and adults, and it is safe to say that none of the food they are offered is suitable.

Joan Ward-Harris *Creature comforts*, 1979

Two beautiful deer came sauntering across the grounds, and stopped and looked me over as if they thought of buying me.

Mark Twain *Letters*, 1925

Beautiful, brown, and unafraid,
Those eyes returned my stare;
And something with neither sound nor name
Passed between us there.

Rachel Field *Meeting*
[As a child she had met a deer that had come to drink at a brook.]

Queen Anne did not think the Forest of Wolmer beneath her royal regard . . . She saw with great complacency and satisfaction the whole herd of red deer brought by the keepers along the vale before her, consisting then of about five hundred head.

Gilbert White *Natural history of Selborne*, 1789

ANTLERS

Red deer are shy animals, and rarely seen except by those familiar with their movements. Sight, smell, and hearing are all acute. They can attain a speed of some thirty-five miles per hour, and it is incredible how a stag with a magnificent set of antlers can run in the forest without getting inextricably caught up in trees and bushes.

   Eric Delderfield   *Second book of true animal stories*, 1972

Red are the stags and hinds by Bo-pit Meadows,
The rutting stags that nightly through the beech-woods
Bell out their challenge, carrying their antlers
Proudly beneath the antlered autumn branches.

   V. Sackville-West   *Beechwoods at Knole*, 1921

The warrior stags, with does and tripping fawns,
Like shadows black upon the throbbing mist
Of evening's rose, flash'd through the singing woods –
Nor timorous, sniffed the spicy, cone-breathed air.

   Isabella Valancy Crawford   *Malcolm's Katie*, 1884

The stag guards his hinds jealously; he is continuously rounding them up into a compact group, and, raising his antlered head high, he proclaims ownership by letting out a fine, wild sound called 'belling'.

   Heather Ames   in *Animals* (RSPCA), 1979

DEER-STALKING

The most propitious day for deer-stalking is a cloudy one . . . When the sky is cloudless and the sun very dazzling, the herd are apt to see you at a great distance, and take alarm.

   John Colquhoun   *The moor and the loch*, 1840
   [Fortunately for the author of the following quotation, the deer did not always reveal this disobliging propensity.]

What a noble beast! What a stretch of antlers! . . . Looking through a tuft of rushes, I had a perfect view of the noble animal, lying on the open hillock . . . I fired at his throat. He dropped to his knees, but was up again in a moment, and went staggering up the hill . . . He stood still with his head lowered, and his eyes bloody and swelled. His mane and all

his coat were dripping with water and blood . . . At last I
went up within twenty yards and shot him through the head.

Charles St John *Wild sports and natural history*,
1846
[The writer appeared to be strangely pleased with himself
over this activity. At about the same period, Prince Albert
was showing a similar interest in noble animals.]

We saw deer as we came lower down, and all of a sudden a
stag was seen quite close by the path; Albert shot him, and he
fell at once. He had very fine horns, a royal on one side . . . As
we were sitting by a tree close to Albert a stag came out, and
Albert killed him at one shot.

Queen Victoria *Our life in the Highlands*, 1868

Albert set off immediately after luncheon, deer-stalking . . .
After waiting some time, we were told in a mysterious
whisper that 'they were coming', and indeed a great herd *did*
appear on the brow of the hill and came running down a good
way, when most provokingly two men who were walking on
the road – which they had no business to have done –
suddenly came in sight, and then the herd all ran back again
and the sport was spoilt.

Queen Victoria *Our life in the Highlands* 1868

DEER IN DISTRESS

To the which place a poor sequester'd stag,
That from the hunter's aim had ta'en a hurt,
Did come to languish; and indeed, my lord,
The wretched animal heav'd forth such groans
That their discharge did stretch his leathern coat
Almost to bursting.

William Shakespeare *As you like it, c.* 1600

When the tiger approaches can the fast-fleeting hind
Repose trust in his footsteps of air?
No! Abandoned he sinks in a trance of despair,
The monster transfixes his prey,
On the sand flows his life-blood away.

P. B. Shelley *Bigotry's victim*, 1811

Mrs Jenkins told me that about 5 a.m. she saw a creature rush
madly into the little stable and then dash out again, hop over

the stone wall into the brook, and away. Two couples of white hounds came hunting down the lane with the keepers . . . She went into the stable and saw by the hoof marks and the mud that the poor hunted creature, in its frantic terror and attempts to escape and hide itself, had climbed up into the manger.

Francis Kilvert *Diary*, 1878

He stands at bay;
And puts his last weak refuge in despair.
The big round tears run down his dappled face;
He groans in anguish; while the growling pack,
Blood happy, hang at his fair jutting chest.

James Thomson *The seasons, autumn*, 1730

Nature in vain his lofty head adorns
With formidable groves of pointed thorns.
Soon as the hounds' fierce clamour strikes his ear
He throws his arms behind, and owns his fear;
He, trembling, safety seeks in every place.

John Leyden *Scottish descriptive poems*, 1802

Elephant

The elephant's a gentleman.

Rudyard Kipling *Oonts*, 1892

If anyone wants to know what elephants are like, they are like people only more so.

Peter Corneille in *Theatreprint*, 1984

The elephant is never won with anger.

Earl of Rochester *Valentinian*, 1683

Thy impudence hath a monstrous beauty, like the hind quarters of an elephant.

J. Elroy Flecker *Hassan*, 1921

STRENGTH AND DELICACY

It has always seemed miraculous to me that these colossal animals can move noiselessly through the bush, and are thus able to surround one without warning.

Joy Adamson *Born free*, 1960

Watch a human being walk through a bush and it is a messy business. Watch an elephant encounter a thicket of twig and thorn, and he seems to flow through it.

Anthony Smith *Throw out two hands*, 1963

The smooth straight telegraph poles are irresistible [to elephants]. They seem to have been provided expressly for pachyderms to rub themselves against. They are not all very firm, and . . . in a single night one strong elephant can bring down a big stretch of telegraph line.

Albert Schweitzer *On the edge of the primeval forest*, 1922

With a wave of his trunk
And a turn of his chin
He can pull down a house,
Or pick up a pin.

Herbert Asquith *The elephant*, 1934

The elephant can with his trunk pick up a sixpence or uproot a tree.

W. Somerset Maugham *The gentleman in the parlour*, 1930

ELEPHANTS AT WORK

When these sagacious creatures are seen at useful work there is a quiet dignity in the way they go about their tasks.

Charles Bertram *A magician in many lands*, 1911

I could see the fun which the elephants derived from rolling the logs into the water and then watching them caught in the stream and floating away.

J. H. Williams *In quest of a mermaid*, 1960

A number of very heavy beams were lashed together and the end of a rope was then thrown to the elephant, which took it into its mouth and wound it twice round its trunk. Unaided and without a keeper, the elephant proceeded to drag the beams to the place where the vessel was under construction.

Father Philippe *Journey to the Orient*, 1669

An elephant with his trunk coiled up will push at one end of a log 35 feet long and weighing three tons, and guide it in and out of the avenues of stacked wood, until he brings it to its destination. A second elephant will then assist, and the two will lift an enormous log to the top of the pile.

Charles Bertram   *A magician in many lands*, 1911

To watch an elephant building a bridge, to see the skill with which the great beasts lifted the huge logs, and the accuracy with which they were coaxed into position, was to realise that the elephant was no mere transport animal but indeed a skilled sapper.

Field-Marshal William Slim   in J. H. Williams, *Elephant Bill*, 1950

Hannibal's elephants could be induced to move but very slowly along the steep and narrow trails [of the Alps]; but wherever they went they made his invading army safe from its enemies, who were unaccustomed to the beasts and afraid to venture too near them.

Livy   *History, c.* 25 BC

ELEPHANT ECCENTRICITIES

Once, in Ceylon, I saw an enormous sacred elephant sit up and beg for a banana; I don't believe it really wanted the banana, it merely knew what was expected of it.

Noel Coward   *Present indicative*, 1937

The elephant, the huge old beast,
is slow to mate;
he finds a female, they show no haste,
they wait.

D. H. Lawrence   *Pansies*, 1929

In order to leave nothing to chance, elephants plaster themselves with mud and dust as a further protection against both heat and flies . . . In the animal kingdom it is not necessary to be thin-skinned to be sensitive.

C. Court Treatt   *Out of the beaten track*, 1930

If he cannot reach with his trunk some part of his body that itches, he doesn't always rub it against a tree; he may pick up a long stick and give himself a good scratch with that instead. If one stick isn't long enough he will look for another that is.

J. H. Williams   *Elephant Bill*, 1950

A resting herd is silent except for two things: elephants snore, and they never stop flapping their ears, even in sleep. The convulsive flapping . . . can be heard for thirty or forty yards.

Ronald McKie *The company of animals*, 1965

One of the mysteries connected with the elephant is that his huge body needs less sleep than anything else that lives. Four or five hours in the night suffice.

Rudyard Kipling *Moti Guj – mutineer*, 1895

When elephants are out of sight of each other they purr. If danger approaches one of them, it stops purring. When the danger has passed the purring is resumed.

Maurice Burton *Just like an animal*, 1978

The noises made by the animals themselves were quite terrifying. One neighed shrilly like a horse, another grunted like a whole herd of pigs, while a third growled deep down in his stomach in the most sinister way.

F. Spencer Chapman *Living dangerously*, 1953

One of them was in the centre of the track, its ears spread out, its trunk extended. I had never dreamed that an elephant could look so big. And now it advanced upon us, squealing as it came.

K. Gandar Dower *The spotted lion*, 1937

There is a widespread belief that an elephant is really afraid of a mouse. The idea makes an obvious appeal to the human love of paradox.

J. H. Williams *Elephant Bill*, 1950
[Doubting the belief, Williams points out that a sneeze would be enough to remove the mouse from the elephant's trunk.]

Th'unwieldy elephant
To make them mirth us'd all his might and wreath'd
His lithe proboscis.

John Milton *Paradise lost*, 1667
[This engaging entertainment was given in the Garden of Eden before Adam and Eve.]

Every herd chooses a leader strong or clever enough to protect it. Occasionally a female is chosen, if she exceeds the

bull elephants in reason and judgment. Whether the leader is
a bull or a cow, once chosen it finds strict obedience in all
members of the herd.

J. E. Tennent *The wild elephant*, 1867

He thought he saw an elephant
That practised on a fife:
He looked again, and found it was
A letter from his wife.

Lewis Carroll *Sylvie and Bruno*, 1889

Did I ever tell you how I shot a wild elephant in my pyjamas.
How he got into my pyjamas I'll never know.

Groucho Marx *Animal crackers* (film)

Elephants loathe little dogs.

Rudyard Kipling *My lord the elephant*, 1895

An elephant is a square animal with a tail in front and behind.

Quoted in **Cecil Hunt** *The best howlers*, 1949

BABY ELEPHANTS

Shmetty felt deprived unless she had a biscuit, although she
had no idea what to do with it, and waved it around, popping
it in and out of her mouth, or even in and out of her ear,
sucking it up in her trunk, until it disintegrated and finally
got blown out in an elephant-sized sneeze.

Daphne Sheldrick *My four-footed family*, 1979

Feeding a [baby] elephant is not easy at the best of times, for
one has to mix gallons, not pints, and the bottle and teat have
to be elephantine as well.

Daphne Sheldrick *My four-footed family*, 1979

I saw the calf back his hind quarters towards his mother's
head. When she felt him she raised her trunk and rested it on
the calf's back; and in this way they moved about the
clearing. It was like a little boy holding his blind mother's
hand and steering her down the street.

J. H. Williams *In quest of a mermaid*, 1960
[The mother elephant had been accidentally blinded by the
juice of a poisonous creeper.]

Ermine

[There is a legend] that if an ermine be encircled with mud it will fastidiously prefer capture to crossing the dirty barrier.

Phil Robinson   *The poets' beasts*, 1885

I will disdain, and from your proffers fly,
As from vile dirt the snowy ermine.

William Cowper   *The task*, 1785

The white flash . . . stopped almost at my feet to look up at me. This was an ermine, exquisitively graceful, fluffy as whipped cream and as creamy white, too, with black tail tip and ear touches, eyes like polished jet, a pink nose, and rounded ears, pink-lined. He sat up, all of eight inches high.

Helen Hoover   *A place in the woods*, 1970

White ermine was meant to express moral purity; white waistcoats were not.

G. K. Chesterton   *What's wrong with the world*, 1910

Field-mouse

Wee, sleekit, cow'rin', tim'rous beastie,
O what a panic's in thy breastie!
Thou need na start awa sae hasty,
Wi' bickering brattle!

Robert Burns   *To a mouse (On turning her up in her nest with the plough, November 1785)*

A field-mouse, disturbed by the point of the ploughshare, goes scrambling over the moving furrow, only to be buried beneath it. You are sorry for him, but . . . the mouse must take his chance.

A. G. Street   *Farmer's glory*, 1932

There are many more of these brown field-mice in the hedges than are suspected to be there; their little bodies slip about so near the surface of the brown earth, the colour of which they resemble, that few notice them.

Richard Jefferies   *Wild life in a southern county*, 1879

Their grand rendezvous seems to be in corn-ricks. A neighbour housed an oat-rick lately, under the thatch of which were assembled near an hundred field-mice.

Gilbert White   *Natural history of Selborne*, 1768

We found a mouse in the chalk quarry today
In a circle of stones and empty oil drums
By the fag end of a fire. There had been
A picnic there: he must have been after the crumbs.

Ian Serraillier   *Anne and the fieldmouse*, 1963

Mice-tracks (in the snow) are very pretty, and look like a sort of fantastic stitching on the coverlet of the snow. One is curious to know what brings these tiny creatures from their retreats; they do not seem to be in search of food.

John Burroughs   *The snow-walkers*, 1893

This autumn I procured the nest of a harvest-mouse, most artificially platted, and composed of the blades of wheat; perfectly round, and about the size of a cricket-ball.

Gilbert White   *Natural history of Selborne*, 1767

Fox

LITTLE RED DOG

The fox, after all, is a little red dog, and he hunts – and eats – the sort of things your dog would hunt and eat if you did not keep him supplied with dog food.

W. Kay Robinson   *Britain's beasts of prey*, 1949

Of all babies of the wild, the fox cub at the age of four weeks is perhaps the most attractive. His eyes have that same wondering look that one sees in very small babies of the human species.

'B.B.'   *Wild lone*, 1938

A little fox, with his face full of a grave sweet intelligence which is as yet undebased by the look of worldly astuteness conspicuous in after-life, is one of the prettiest sights in the world.

Colonel E. B. Hamley   *Our poor relations*, 1872

A word of sympathy for the vixen that will run before the hounds with a cub in her mouth for miles and miles . . . a word, in fact, for the pretty little beast of prey that, but for encroaching farmsteads and game-preservers, would be abundantly content to live entirely upon wild birds and animals.

Phil Robinson   *The poets' beasts*, 1885

The fox's hunting is quite as legitimate and a great deal more necessary to his existence than is that of the gamekeeper.

Konrad Lorenz   *King Solomon's ring*, 1952

I have found, when talking to farmers, that the visual evidence of a fox killing a lamb or a sheep is almost non-existent. Eating is no proof of killing.

Jane Ratcliffe   *Fly high, run free*, 1979

A writer evidently conversant with the natural history of foxes declares that the rat stands first in Reynard's menu. He adds that foxes are very fond of grapes; and so the author of the well-known fable knew what he was about.

Illustrated sporting and dramatic news, 4 Oct. 1890

Sometimes I heard the foxes as they ranged over the snow crusts in search of a partridge or other game, barking raggedly . . . Sometimes one came near to my window, attracted by my light, barked a vulpine curse at me, and then retreated.

H. D. Thoreau   *Walden*, 1854

A fox barks away up the next mountain, and I imagine I can almost see him sitting there, in his furs, looking down in my direction. As I listen, one answers him from behind the woods.

John Burroughs   *Nature's diary*, 1893

Gracefullest leaper, the dappled fox-cub
Curves over brambles with berries and buds,
Light as a bubble that flies from the tub
Whisked by the laundry-wife out of her suds.
Wavy he comes, woolly, all at his ease.

George Meredith   *Young reynard*, 1887

FOX ABOUT TOWN

Foxes, protected for hunts in many districts, are common. As in other parts of the country, some of them have taken to town life, and often visit or even take up residence in suburban gardens.

Ralph Whitlock *Wildlife in Wessex*, 1976

I recently . . . saw a large fox trot past [my friend's] window and go down to a compost heap in broad daylight. I was assured that it was quite wild and that it came regularly to the bird table in search of any scraps.

Phil Drabble *Pleasing pets*, 1975

The collapse of the rabbit population . . . created the 'commuting fox' which lives on the urban fringe and travels into city centres at night to scavenge for food.

James Preston in *Daily Telegraph*, 22 Aug. 1983

FOXES AT PLAY

When the old foxes were not about, the young, half-grown rabbits would freely mix and play with the little foxes . . . pursuing one another round and round.

W. H. Hudson *A shepherd's life*, 1910

I watched a fox on the lower slope of Beachy Cove Mountain playing with an almost perfectly round beach stone. He would carry it to the top of a little sloping mouse-meadow, drop it, then give it a head start before taking after it and trying to catch it as it tumbled downhill.

Harold Horwood *The foxes of Beachy Cove*, 1967

A vixen and three cubs were sitting on their haunches in a rough line. A huge dog fox . . . barking furiously as he gained speed, galloped towards them. When only a few feet from them he suddenly rolled over and rolled across the grass several times. He got up, shook himself, and repeated the game.

James Preston in *Daily Telegraph*, 21 Jan. 1984

FOX-HUNT

Just at close of day
There by the comet's light we saw the fox

Rush from the alders, nor relax in speed
Until he trod the pathway of his sires
Under the hoary crag of Comioy.

W. S. Landor   *Fiesolan musings*, 1846
[Comioy, or Cwmyoy, is in the Black Mountains, Wales.]

I heard no alien stir in the friendly wood,
But the fox's sculpted attitude was tense
With scenting, listening, with a seventh sense
Flaring to the alert.

Phoebe Hesketh   *The fox*, 1958

There is a field through which I often pass,
Thick overspread with moss and silky grass . . .
Where oft the bitch-fox hides her hapless brood,
Reserved to solace many a neighbouring squire,
That he may follow them through brake and brier,
Contusion hazarding of neck or spine,
Which rural gentlemen call sport divine.

William Cowper   *The needless alarm*, 1794

Sir Roger's stable-doors are patched with noses that belonged
to foxes of the Knight's own hunting down. He showed me
one of them that cost him about fifteen hours riding, carried
him through half a dozen counties, killed him a brace of
geldings, and lost above half his dogs.

Joseph Addison   *The Spectator*, 1711
[Sir Roger de Coverley, in most respects a worthy
gentleman, was squire of his village.]

In order to establish his reputation [as a fox-hunter] Sir
Roger has secretly sent for great numbers of foxes out of
other counties, which he used to turn loose about the country
by night, that he might the better signalize himself in their
destruction the next day.

Eustace Budgell   *The Spectator*, 1711

A brushing fox in yonder wood
Secure to find we seek;
For why? I carried sound and good
A cartload there last week.

Henry Fielding   *Hunting song*

It seemed a shame to be taking those cubs away from the
mother and transporting them to some district where the

hunt was getting short of foxes, for that was the sole idea of digging them out – just that they might be hunted to death some other where.

Fred Kitchen *Brother to the ox*, 1942

'If I could but go to the kennel now, get out the 'ounds, find my fox, have a good chivey, and kill him, for no day is good to me without blood.'

R. S. Surtees *Handley Cross*, 1843
[Mr Jorrocks is a keen cockney fox-hunter.]

Here, as he ran to the huntsman's yelling,
The fox first felt that the pace was telling;
His body and lungs seemed all grown old,
His legs less certain, his heart less bold.

John Masefield *Reynard the fox*, 1919

A fox, in a well-supplied district, is seldom hunted more than twice in a season . . . Hunting with hounds is cruel, however, and man knows it to be cruel.

'B.B.' *Wild lone*, 1938

The fox
Hangs his silver tongue in the world of noise
Over his spattering paws. Will he run
Till his muscles suddenly turn to iron,
Till blood froths his mouth as his lungs tatter,
Till his feet are raw blood-sticks and his tail
Trails thin as a rat's?

Ted Hughes *Foxhunt*, 1979

So then, men vaunt in vaine, which say they hunt the Foxe
To kepe their neighbours poultry free, and to defend their flockes –
When they themselves can spoyle more profit in an houre
Than Reynard rifles in a yere, when he doth most devoure.

George Turberville *The noble art of venerie*, 1575

When a fox makes for our area the hounds are called off, and the fox, sidling along the hedges of our fields to the impenetrable brambles and thorn trees which slope steeply to the sea, is safe.

Derek Tangye *A cat in the window*, 1962

If foxes, like women, had a vote I think they would vote
unanimously for the keeping of fox-hunting.

Colonel Sir Lancelot Rolleston   quoted in **Michael
Bateman,** *This England*

FOX AT BAY

Mrs Fand wore a fox round her wrinkled throat;
He was killed at dawn as he snarled his threat
In a bracken-brake where the mist lay wet.

Stella Gibbons   *Collected poems,* 1950

The keeper was walking up a deep dry ditch when his spaniel
and a retriever suddenly 'chopped' a fox, and got him at bay
in a corner, when he turned, and in an instant laid the spaniel
helpless and dying and severely handled the retriever . . . The
keeper imprudently attempted to seize him, but got the sharp
white teeth clean through his hand.

Richard Jefferies   *The gamekeeper at home,* 1878
[To 'chop' is to catch a victim before it is fairly away from
cover. As the French say, 'The fox is a wicked animal – it
defends itself.']

I watched a fox break cover for some rocks with three jackals
in pursuit. They cornered the fox in a shallow niche in some
rocks. Whereupon the jackals set to and had a terrific free for
all, presumably to decide which of them should go in for the
kill . . . The fox suddenly sprang, cleared the jackals' backs
with a foot or more to spare, and was a hundred yards away
before they realized.

Brian Stuart   *Desert adventure,* 1954

Giraffe

The giraffes browse
With stately heads among the forest boughs.

James Montgomery   *The West Indies,* 1809

Under a group of trees some little distance away, a herd of
giraffe were standing, their heads among the leaves.

Cherry Kearton   *The animals came to drink,* 1932

I think the giraffe is the handsomest of all the animals. As I
see it, he is the aristocrat of Africa . . . a vegetarian by
conviction, a good mother, and entirely devoid of the
offensive spirit.

C. Court Treatt   *Out of the beaten track*, 1930

Giraffes communicate with each other by the way they hold
their necks, the position of their bodies, and the posture of
the tail.

Maurice Burton   *Just like an animal*, 1978

The tail of the giraffe looks like an artificially constructed fly-
flapper; it seems at first incredible that this could have been
adapted by successive slight modifications for so trifling an
object as driving away flies.

Charles Darwin   *On the origin of species*, 1895

Giraffes defend themselves with their very powerful kick.

Oxford junior encyclopedia, 1949

The lion, instead of advancing, began slowly to circle round
the giraffe, never encroaching on the thirty yards of ground
that separated them . . . If he came within range, the giraffe's
front foot would suddenly shoot out with enormous force.

Cherry Kearton   *The animals came to drink*, 1932

Daisy carefully tapped the ball with the front of a fore-hoof.
It rolled a little way across the yard. Daisy walked lazily after
it and played it forward another few yards . . . The ball rolled
gently over the grass with the three giraffes in dignified
pursuit.

David Taylor   *Next panda, please*, 1982

No living creature in this world runs as the giraffe does. It
moves its legs in pairs on either side, first the right side
forward, then the left, and this imparts a singular undulating
motion to the huge beast. It flows across the countryside with
the delayed rhythm of a film in slow motion.

Alan Moorehead   *No room in the ark*, 1959

Each time I look at a giraffe
Somehow it makes me want to laugh.

Anon.

Gnu

I know two things about the gnu,
But both are probably untrue.

   Anon.

To watch these idiotic creatures prancing, gyrating, and
snorting, their tails curling up over their backs, was one of the
funniest sights I have seen . . . Some of it resembled folk
dancing.

   Gerald Durrell   *Beasts in my belfry*, 1973

An animal of South Africa, which in its domesticated state
resembles a horse, a buffalo, and a stag. In its wild condition
it is something like a thunderbolt, an earthquake, and a
cyclone.

   Ambrose Bierce   *The devil's dictionary*, 1911

Hare

The most typical animal of the open downland is
undoubtedly the hare. Open country is its natural habitat. It
lies in forms, camouflaged by its russet coat, in fields so bare
that they seem to offer no inch of cover. There its young are
born, eyes open, completely coated in fur and able to run.

   Ralph Whitlock   *Wildlife in Essex*, 1976

In Summer or Spring time you shall find hares in Corn-fields
and open places, not sitting in bushes for fear of snakes. In
winter they love tufts of thorns and brambles, near houses.

   R. H.   *The school of recreation*, 1696

A hare, grey as the grass, leaped up and dived into the wind,
the mist, and the rain.

   Edward Thomas   *Light and twilight*, 1911

The hare limp'd trembling through the frozen grass.

   John Keats   *The eve of St Agnes*, 1819

Thick tussocks of old grass are conspicuous . . . From behind
one of these tussocks a hare starts, his black-tipped ears erect,
his long hinder limbs throwing him almost like a grasshopper
over the sward.

   Richard Jefferies   *The open air*, 1885

HARE MAGIC

Hares were held in much esteem among the ancient Britons as magic-working animals. Caesar says that they made use of hares for purposes of divination . . . Augurs might divine whether the omens were good or evil from the turnings and windings made by the frightened animal.

F. T. Elworthy   *The evil eye*, 1895

There are few above the age of threescore and ten who are not perplexed [upset] at a hare crossing their path.

Thomas Browne   *Pseudodoxia epidemica*, 1646

If a poor timorous hare but crosse the way,
Morus will keep his chamber all the day.

Francis Quarles   *Divine emblems*, 1635

Besides the ancient superstition attached to the crossing of a path by a hare, there is also a belief that the running of one along the street or mainway of a village portends a fire to some house in the immediate vicinity.

Notes and queries, 1859

A witch is a kind of hare
And marks the weather
As the hare doth.

Ben Jonson   *The sad shepherd*, 1641

'When I go but into my closet I am afraid, for I see now and then a hare, which my conscience giveth me is a witch, or some witch's spirit, she stareth so upon me.'

George Gifford   *A dialogue concerning witches and witchcraftes*, 1593

In a good many places it is believed that witches are transformed after death into hares; and a lady wrote to me from the Isle of Man that she could not get her servants to eat hare, because it might be the body of some old woman transformed.

S. Baring-Gould   *A book of folklore*, 1913

Now I am at a losse to know whether it be my hare's foot
which is my preservative against wind, for I never had a fit of
the collique since I wore it.

Samuel Pepys   *Diary*, 1665

HUNTED HARE

Each outcry of the hunted hare
A fibre from the brain does tear

William Blake   *Auguries of innocence*, c. 1801

Poor is the triumph o'er the timid hare!
Scared from the corn, and now to some lone seat
Retired.

James Thomson   *The seasons, autumn*, 1730

The hare
Though timorous of heart, and hard beset
By death in various forms, dark snares, and dogs,
And more unpitying men, the garden seeks,
Urged on by fearless want.

James Thomson   *The seasons, winter*, 1726

From brake to brake she flies, and visits all
Her well-known haunts . . . each eager hound exerts
His utmost speed . . . till round enclosed
By all the greedy pack, with infant screams
She yields her breath, and there, reluctant, dies.

William Somerville   *The chase*, 1735

The kill is generally the most painful part of the whole
business because, in the first place, the cries of the hare are
often piercing and piteous in the extreme, resembling those
of a child in agony.

'Stonehenge' (J. H. Walsh)   *British rural sports*, 1856

Thanks to her senses five
This charmer is alive;
Who cheated the loud pack,
Biting steel, poacher's sack;
Among the steep rocks
Outwitted the fanged fox.

Lilian Bowes Lyon   *The white hare*, 1934

Inhuman man! curse on thy barb'rous art,
And blasted be thy murder-aiming eye:
May never pity soothe thee with a sigh,
Nor ever pleasure glad thy cruel heart!

Robert Burns *On seeing a wounded hare limp by me*, 1789

HARES ON HIND LEGS

It is amusing to see two of these animals drumming each other; they stand on their hind legs (which are very long) like a dog taught to beg, and strike with the fore pads as if boxing . . . Round and round they go like a couple waltzing, now one giving ground and then the other, the forelegs striking all the while with marvellous rapidity.

Richard Jefferies *Wild life in a southern county*, 1879

It is fascinating to remember the authenticated story of hares, which, standing on their hind legs, dance in circles of several at a time, during certain seasons. I have met countrymen who have seen this.

Pennethorne Hughes *Witchcraft*, 1952

As we went along we could see the Patagonian hare racing us along the road – a delightful creature who sits up kangaroo-fashion on his hind legs to watch you go by.

Jacquie Durrell *Beasts in my bed*, 1967

QUITE CONTRARY

Would rather run up-hill than down-hill;
Would rather look backwards than forwards;
Escapes by going the long way round,
Or by lying still.

John Heath-Stubbs *The hare*, 1965

The hare's eyes are so much to the side of its head that it can actually see better behind than in front. This is a useful defence against unexpected attacks.

Jane Ratcliffe *Fly high, run free*, 1979

Thou madde March hare!

John Skelton *Replycacion agaynst certaine yong scolers, c.* 1526

Hedgehog

Thorny hedgehogs be not seen . . .
Come not near our fairy queen.

William Shakespeare *A midsummer night's dream,*
c. 1595

HEDGEHOG IN THE HOME

Years ago, when I lived at Weybridge, there was a hedgehog
that came now and then into the house and drank from a
saucer set before him.

Eric Parker *Surrey*, 1947

A visitor would have been astonished to see a hedgehog
calmly lying full length in front of the fire, as if he had been a
cat long established in the home.

The Times anthology, 1933

A hedgehog used to give us tremendous fun by hiding under
Nanny's chair . . . One day he suddenly decided to go
exploring. Slowly he crept up Nanny's foot and began to
crawl up her leg, when she awoke with an unearthly yell.

Barbara Woodhouse *Talking to animals*, 1954

HEDGEHOG ON THE LAWN

If I pass during some nocturnal blackness, mothy and warm,
When the hedgehog travels furtively over the lawn,
One may say, 'He strove that such innocent creatures should
come to no harm.'

Thomas Hardy *Afterwards*, 1917

The hedgehog underneath the plantain bores.

Alfred Tennyson *Aylmer's field*, 1864

The manner in which they eat the roots of the plantain in my
grass walk is very curious: with their upper mandible, which
is much longer than their lower, they bore under the plant,
and so eat the root off upwards. In this respect they are
serviceable, as they destroy a very troublesome weed; but
they deface the walks in some measure by digging little round
holes.

Gilbert White *Natural history of Selborne*, 1770

QUILLS AND PRICKLES

The shepherd's lurcher, who, among the crags,
Had to his joy unearthed a hedgehog, teased
His coiled-up prey with barkings turbulent.

William Wordsworth *The prelude*, 1798–1805

From a hollow tree the hedgehog
With his sleepy eyes looked at him,
Shot his shining quills like arrows,
Saying, with a drowsy murmur,
Through the tangle of his whiskers,
'Take my quills, O Hiawatha!'

H. W. Longfellow *The song of Hiawatha*, 1855

It is hardly necessary to deny the popular belief that the
animal can shoot out its quills like so many arrows; the notion
has arisen from the fact that when the animal erects its spines,
loose ones sometimes fall out.

Chambers's encyclopedia, 1923
[The denial is relevant both to hedgehogs and porcupines.]

All wild hedgehogs have a great many fleas, largely because
they find it impossible to scratch their own skin or back and
sides because of the prickles. If you watch a hedgehog closely
you will see fleas crawling about among the spines. Don't be
put off. These fleas seem peculiar to hedgehogs and will not
bite people.

Phil Drabble *Pleasing pets*, 1975

He lies like a hedgehog rolled up the wrong way,
Tormenting himself with his prickles.

Thomas Hood *Miss Kilmansegg and her precious
leg*, 1841–3

Pliny in his time had a story about hedgehogs rolling on
windfall apples so as to impale the fruits on their spines . . . It
is just conceivable and indeed may occasionally happen that
ripe fruit falls off a tree on to a hedgehog's back and sticks
there. But that it purposefully and systematically carries fruit
on its prickles can be nothing but a legend.

Konrad Herter *Hedgehogs*, 1965

No doubt their spines are soft and flexible at the time of their birth, but it is plain that they soon harden, for these little pigs (five or six days old) had such stiff prickles on their backs as would easily have fetched blood.

Gilbert White   *Natural history of Selborne*, 1770

The hedgehog has only one instinct as far as self-preservation is concerned, and that is to roll into a ball of protective spines. This is all very well, but spines weren't designed to combat speeding motorcars . . . Unless motorists slow down and toot their horns (it does work, believe me) the hedgehog is going to join the ranks of the vanished.

Percy Edwards   *Percy Edwards' country book*, 1980

HEDGEHOG IMMUNITY

A hedgehog observed to have been stung by fifty-two bees seemed to suffer no inconvenience.

Konrad Herter   *Hedgehogs*, 1965

A viper struck the hedgehog two or three times in the face, and meant to do business, as at that moment the hedgehog was munching at the attacking viper's tail. The hedgehog did not suffer in the least.

Frank Buckland   *notes to* White's *Natural history of Selborne*, 1876

Hippopotamus

HIPPO IN THE WATER

During the first weeks of his existence the little hippo spent most of his time lying asleep near the hot-water pipes, but he could swim almost from birth and usually suckled under water.

Helen M. Sidebotham   *Mysteries of the zoo*, 1927

We met a herd of fifteen hippos, who soon plunged into the water on our approach, but a quite young one remained amusing itself on the sandbank, and would not obey its mother when she called to it.

Albert Schweitzer   *On the edge of the primeval forest*, 1922

Albert Schweitzer & Hippo.

The hippopotamus amidst the flood
Flexile and active as the smallest swimmer,
But on the bank ill-balanced and infirm.

    James Montgomery   *The world before the flood*,
1812

Another hippo lay lazily munching in the shadows, a large
water-lily drooping from the corner of his mouth giving him
the appearance of some strange prehistoric Gilbertian
aesthete.

    C. Court Treatt   *Out of the beaten track*, 1930

Most of the day he appears to do nothing very much except
lie there close to the surface of the water, gently submerging
and rising again, and he discloses himself from quite a long
way off by a faint smell of drains.

    Alan Moorehead   *No room in the ark*, 1959

HEAVY HIPPO

It has often been stated that aside from the elephant, the
white rhinoceros is the largest living land mammal. The
authors of such positive statements seem to have forgotten
that overgrown pig, the hippopotamus. In spite of dumpy
legs and a shoulder height of five feet . . . the weight of the
hippo is remarkable. One in the London Zoo is stated to have
weighed 8,600 pounds.

    Osmond P. Breland   *Animal friends and foes*, 1958

I put on a small torch and raised it. There was the bull
[hippo], all three tons of it, standing stock still about ten
yards from us. I kept the torch off its eyes and it came
forward another few yards. I suddenly remembered the story
I had been told of a hippo crunching up the bonnet of a car by
the simple process of biting it.

    Ernest Neal   *Uganda quest*, 1971

HIPPO HUMOUR

The hippo has got huge warts on his hind feet, and hates
them. If ever I saw a weary cynic I saw the creature in him.

    Stopford A. Brooke   *Diary*, 1899

I have seen the hippopotamus both asleep and awake; and I can assure you that, awake or asleep, he is the ugliest of the works of God.

    T. B. Macaulay   *Letters*, 1850

A hippopotamus had a bride
Of rather singular beauty,
And when he lay down at her side
'Twas out of love, not duty.

    J. H. Wheelock   *Hippopotomothalamion*, 1936

I had a hippopotamus; I kept him in a shed,
And fed him upon vitamins and vegetable bread.

    Patrick Barrington   *I had a hippopotamus*, 1934

He thought he saw a Banker's Clerk
Descending from a bus:
He looked again, and found it was
A Hippopotamus.
'If this should stay to dine,' he said,
'There won't be much for us!'

    Lewis Carroll   *Sylvie and Bruno*, 1889

Hyena

Scorning all the taming arts of man,
The keen hyena, fellest of the fell.

    James Thomson   *The seasons, summer*, 1727

The cowardice of the hyena makes us forget its enormous strength . . . This is not restricted to biting. An adult spotted hyena can carry off a full-sized ass.

    Harmsworth natural history, 1910

The Nairobi National Park lies so close to Nairobi that the hyenas are said to come scavenging through the city streets at night.

    Alan Moorehead   *No room in the ark*, 1959

Only the fierce hyena stalks
Throughout the city's desolate walks
At midnight, and his carnage plies.
Woe to the half-dead wretch who meets

The glaring of those large blue eyes
Amid the darkness of the streets.

Thomas Moore *Poetical works*, 1840–2

While waiting for the moon to sink,
We saw a wild hyena slink
About a new-made grave, and then
Begin to excavate its brink.

Ambrose Bierce *The devil's dictionary*, 1911

Hyenas would moan as they slunk along the darkened banks
of the forest streams, nosing for death.

Llewelyn Powys *Black laughter*, 1924

Once I awoke to hear the bone-chilling howl of a hyena, close
to the house. Hyenas were said to be cowards, but in their
midnight howlings there was something intimate, knowing,
and sly, as if they were saying; it will be your turn one day.

Elspeth Huxley *The flame trees of Thika*, 1959
[An autobiographical record of childhood in Kenya.]

The laughing noise they make is nothing to do with mirth. It
is a kind of squeal which they use when they are frustrated or
frightened. It is a high falsetto cackle which sounds more like
a woman in trouble than in a mood of pleasure. It is eerie and
sinister.

Mervyn Cowie *Fly, vulture*, 1961

Hyenas have amazing savagery and determination. One alone
will drive away a cheetah . . . Two hyenas will force a leopard
to abandon a kill; a dozen of them will defeat a lion.

Alan Moorehead *No room in the ark*, 1959

A few months previously a man had had his foot chewed off
. . . His error had been to camp out beneath neither tent nor
mosquito net, and to have a large hole in his sleeping-bag. A
passing hyena had seen a whitish piece of flesh pointing into
the air. He then took a grab at it.

Anthony Smith *Throw out two hands*, 1963

Hyrax

I have never heard ten navvies being strangled
simultaneously, but I now know what they would sound like.

How that creature's tortured windpipe survived those laryngeal lacerations I do not know.

Anthony Smith *Throw out two hands*, 1963

Her excretory habits were peculiar; rock hyraxes always use the same place, for preference the edge of a rock; at home Pati invariably perched herself on the rim of the lavatory seat, and thus situated presented a comical sight.

Joy Adamson *Born free*, 1960

Jackal

The jackal's cry
Resounds like sylvan revelry.

Reginald Heber *Poetical works*, 1812

The jackal's troop, in gather'd cry,
Bay'd from afar complainingly,
With a mix'd and mournful sound,
Like crying babe and beaten hound.

Lord Byron *Siege of Corinth*, 1816

I had an orphaned jackal puppy, whose mother had been beaten to death in a trap for the sake of her skin . . . She was a shy, red, foxy thing who belonged far more to the night of the dark forest than she ever did to me . . . Nevertheless she accorded me some measure of affection inasmuch as I was the only person she *didn't* bite.

June Kay *The thirteenth moon*, 1970

Jaguar

As I was walking quietly along I saw a large jet-black animal come out of the forest about twenty yards before me. It was a fine black jaguar. In the middle of the road he turned his head, and for an instant paused and looked steadily at me. But having, I supposed, other business to attend to, he walked steadily on, and disappeared in the thicket.

Alfred Russell Wallace *Travels on the Amazon*, 1853

The jaguar's name is derived from an Indian word *yaquara*, that means 'he who kills with one leap'. The name fits: the jaguar never has to leap more than once.

Rosamund Fisher *My jungle babies*, 1979

About five yards away and a foot or so from the ground a couple of yellow lights blazed into being. They were steady and unwinking, a few inches apart . . . I was now fairly certain that a jaguar was crouching in the shadows . . . Suddenly I had a kind of inspiration. I began to sing 'Show me the way to go home' . . . Towards the end of the second verse the lights disappeared quite silently into the forest.

Julian Duguid *Green hell*, 1931

Kangaroo

The kangaroo, it has always seemed to me, is Exhibit A among the evidence supporting the contention of some that Nature has a grotesque and lovely sense of humour.

James Thurber *Lanterns and lances*, 1961

Old Jumpety-Bumpety-Hop-and-Go-One
Was lying asleep on his side in the sun.
This old kangaroo, he was whisking the flies
With his long glossy tail from his ears and his eyes.

Anon.

At break of day they set out in search of game, and saw four animals, two of which were chased by Mr Banks's greyhound, but they greatly outstripped him in speed. It was observed that they leaped or bounded forward on two legs instead of running on four.

A. Kippis *Voyages of Captain Cook*, 1788

So she wistfully, sensitively sniffs the air, and then turns and goes off in slow sad leaps
On the long flat skis of her legs,
Steered and propelled by that steel-strong snake of a tail.

D. H. Lawrence *Kangaroo*, 1922

Before he had time to realize what was happening, I had
grabbed him by the tail. Powerful as they can be, kangaroos
are helpless if you can get them by the tail and hold on tight.

Terry Murphy   *Some of my best friends are*
animals, 1979

Kangaroos are a nuisance on three or four stations [in
Western Australia], where they are as numerous as sheep.
They eat grass closer to the roots than sheep, and lessen the
carrying capacity of the ground.

John Kirwan   in *The Times anthology*, 1933

When dogs corner a kangaroo he will often make a break,
grab the leading dog in his forearms, and bound away to the
nearest water-hole to drown him. If the dog is not quickly
rescued, the kangaroo keeps pushing him under until he
drowns.

Lowell Thomas   *Sir Hubert Wilkins*, 1961

Lemur

I saw in the middle of the clearing, standing beside a low
flowering bush, three small white figures. They were busily
plucking the petals from the bush and with both hands
cramming them into their mouths. Then George . . . trod on
a twig . . . Immediately they were off, leaping along the
ground with their long hind legs together and their short
arms held in front of them, like people competing in a sack
race.

David Attenborough   *Zoo quest to Madagascar*, 1961

Leopard

The lively-shining leopard, speckled o'er
With many a spot, the beauty of the waste.

James Thomson   *The seasons, summer*, 1727

If strolling forth, a beast you view
Whose hide with spots is peppered,
As soon as she has leapt on you
You'll know it is a leopard.

Carolyn Wells   *How to tell the wild animals*, 1920

There is a hair-trigger ferocity about the leopards . . .
No animal, not even the lion, has such an implacable gaze.

Alan Moorehead *No room in the ark*, 1959

Leopards have a particular liking for the flesh of dogs.

Richard Lydekker in *Harmsworth natural history*,
1910

Leopards are cunning beasts, and will lie quietly until you are
almost on top of them.

J. A. Hunter *Hunter*, 1952

A leopard, unlike a lion, is vindictive, and a leopard when
wounded will fight to a finish, no matter how many chances
he has to make his escape . . . He claws and bites without
stopping.

Carl Akeley *Lions, gorillas, and their neighbours*,
1933

The leopard is apt to fight back when attacked.
Sportsmen with guns feel that this is very unsporting of it.

Anon.

I switched on my torch. There, within two feet of me, was the
face of a leopard . . . I gave a loud shout and at the same time
threw a coat into the leopard's face.

Mervyn Cowie *Fly, vulture*, 1961

As for being bitten on the bottom by a leopard, that was sheer
foolishness on my part. I was clambering among a pile of
rocks when I saw a dead buck on a ledge below me. I jumped
down without realising that it had obviously been dragged
there by some cat . . . The leopard took one startled nip and
then pushed off.

Alan Root quoted in *Telegraph Sunday Magazine*,
12 Oct. 1980

It seems impossible for cats to make an ugly or undignified
movement, and I would say that the leopard in motion is the
most beautiful sight of all.

James Alldiss *Animals as friends*, 1973

Lion

Wouldst thou view the lion's den?

  Thomas Pringle *The lion and the giraffe*, 1834

Dar'st thou then
To beard the lion in his den?

  Walter Scott *Marmion*, 1808

THE LION'S ROAR

At night he heard the lion roar.

  H. W. Longfellow *The slave's dream*, 1842

Snug: Have you the lion's part written?
Quince: You may do it extempore, for it is nothing but roaring.

  William Shakespeare *A midsummer night's dream*, c. 1595

So have I heard on Afric's burning shore
A hungry lion give a grievous roar.

  W. B. Rhodes *Bombastes furioso*, 1810

The lion, as is generally known, only roars when out hunting, but when that roar does make its appearance the whole air rings with it.

  C. Court Treatt *Out of the beaten track*, 1930

Like the roar
Of some pain'd desert lion, who all day
Hath trail'd the hunter's javelin in his side.

  Matthew Arnold *Sohrab and Rustum*, 1853

The growling continued until it got on our nerves. There is something uncanny in the sound of a lion growling when you cannot see the animal, but know it is probably within fifteen or twenty yards of you.

  A. Radclyffe Dugmore *Camera adventures in the African wild*, 1910

A lion then with self-provoking smart
(His rebel tail scourging his noble part)

Calls up his courage; then begins to roar
And charge his foes.

Edmund Waller   *To my lord of Falkland*, 1639

How carefully the poets have credited the fiction of the lion
finding it necessary to exasperate itself up to the necessary
point of fury by lashing its own body with its tail.

Phil Robinson   *The poets' beasts*, 1885

TERROR OF THE JUNGLE

Loose-limbed, he slouches shambling in the cool;
Head down, hide rippling over lazy might;
Thoughtful and terrible he leaves the pool –
Shumba the Lion, passing to the night.

Kingsley Fairbridge   *Veld verse*, 1909

I saw the lion just in the act of springing upon me. He caught
my shoulder as he sprang and we both came to the ground
below together. Growling horribly, close to my ear, he shook
me as a terrier does a rat. The shock produced a stupor,
similar to that which seems to be felt by a mouse after the first
shake of a cat.

David Livingstone   *The Zambesi*, 1865

In the Zambesi district of Africa the belief is held that the
souls of departed chiefs enter into lions and render them
sacred.

William J. Fielding   *Strange superstitions*, 1945

The man that did sell the lion's skin
While the beast lived, was killed with hunting him.

William Shakespeare   *Henry V*, 1599

The lions roaring after their prey: do seek their meat from
God.
The sun ariseth, and they get them away together: and lay
them down in their dens.

Book of Common Prayer, Psalms, 1552

The night before, a lion had jumped the twelve-foot boma
that surrounded the village, seized a cow, and leaped back
over the barrier with the cow in his mouth. I know this feat

sounds incredible, as the lion weighed no more than four
hundred pounds and the cow probably weighed twice that.

   J. A. Hunter   *Hunter*, 1952

The lion is the beast to fight:
He leaps along the plain,
And if you run with all your might.
He runs with all his mane.

   A. Quiller-Couch   *Sage counsel*, 1929

LION CUBS

Lion cubs are always enchanting, but one of these was
particularly so. He had a perfectly round teddy-bear face,
equally round, solemn blue eyes, and a silly habit of sitting
with one front paw bent at the ankle as if he were
demonstrating model shoes.

   June Kay   *The thirteenth moon*, 1970

We had not gone far before Marquis, loping along happily,
spotted a little rabbit . . . For a long minute they stared at
each other, the African lion and the English rabbit. Then
Marquis broke the spell in an embarrassingly ignoble
manner. He gave a little yelp and scampered behind me for
safety.

   Mary Chipperfield   *Lions on the lawn*, 1971
   [Marquis was a two-month-old lion cub.]

THE GENTLE LION

The Lion alone of all wild beasts is gentle to those who
humble themselves unto him, and will not touch any such
upon their submission, but spareth what creatures soever lie
prostrate before him.

   Pliny the Elder   *Natural history*, trans. 1601

After knowing Albert for only three days I realized that
Pliny's description did not fit him . . . Anyone who had
attempted to 'lie prostrate' in front of him would have
received a bite in the back of the neck.

   Gerald Durrell   *Beasts in my belfry*, 1973

Elsa's fame had spread far and wide, and a party of American
sportsmen paid us a visit specially to film her. She entertained

them royally . . . She climbed a tree, played in the river, hugged me, joined us for tea, and behaved in such a docile way that none of our guests could believe that shortly before they arrived she had been equally at ease in the company of wild lions.

Joy Adamson *Born free*, 1960

Evidently lions breed like rabbits, and, as the ranch is already up to capacity, the lionesses are on contraceptive pills.

Tim Heald in *Telegraph Sunday Magazine*, 18 Dec. 1983
[The ranch is run by the Hedrens. See p. 3]

The lion now forgets to thirst for blood:
There might you see him sporting in the sun
Beside the blameless kid; his claws are sheath'd,
His teeth are harmless.

P. B. Shelley *The daemon of the world*, 1815
[Shelley is looking forward to a future as yet unrealized.]

The lion shall eat straw like the ox.

Bible *Isaiah*, 1611

At that very moment a pride of lions emerged from the bush ten yards away and proceeded to walk slowly towards the immobilized vehicle . . . almost with gentle amusement, rather as if they were visitors to the Zoo and we the creatures behind bars.

Peregrine Worsthorne in *Sunday Telegraph*, 15 Jan. 1984
[In a Kenyan game preserve.]

When a lion shakes his dreadful mane,
And angry grows – if he that first took pain
To tame its youth approach the haughty beast,
It bends to him, but frights away the rest.

Edmund Waller *A panegyric to my lord protector*, 1654

Sir George Davis one day went to see the lions of the Duke of Tuscany. There was one which the keepers could not tame, but no sooner did Sir George . . . enter the cage when the creature licked his face, wagged its tail, and fawned like a dog.

Sir George told the Duke that he had brought up this lion,
but as it grew older . . . he sold it.

   E. Cobham Brewer   *The reader's handbook*, 1880

Llama

The Llama is a woolly sort of fleecy hairy goat,
With an indolent expression and an undulating throat.

   Hilaire Belloc   *The llama*, 1897

These South American relatives of the camel have an
unpleasant habit of spitting at visitors.

   Helen M. Sidebotham   *Mysteries of the zoo*, 1927

Lynx

A fierce lynx, with fiery glare.

   John Gay   *Fables*, 1727

I must needs o' the sudden prove myself a lynx
And look the heart, that stone-wall, through and through.

   Robert Browning   *The ring and the book*, 1868–9

Lynxes do not hesitate to avail themselves of their
opportunities, and this with such wastefulness that they will
kill far more sheep than they eat. But then beasts do not know
any better. When they get amongst lambs they are like
children among daisies.

   Phil Robinson   *The poets' beasts*, 1885

The Canadian lynx is a formidable animal, with a strange
habit of trailing a human being for miles – though this is
apparently more through curiosity than with any idea of
harming the man.

   Oxford junior encyclopedia, 1949

Mole

Well said, old mole! canst work i' the earth so fast?

   William Shakespeare   *Hamlet*, 1604

Death is still working like a mole
And digs my grave.

George Herbert   *The temple*, 1634

Who hath not loiter'd in a green churchyard,
And let his spirit, like a demon mole,
Work through the clayey soil and gravel hard,
To see skull, coffin'd bones, and funeral stole.

John Keats   *Isabella*, 1820

We feel at every step
One foot half sunk in hillocks green and soft,
Raised by the mole, the miner of the soil.

William Cowper   *The task*, 1785

Moles are of great service; they eat up the worms that eat the
grass . . . The grass where the moles have been is always the
best for cows.

Frank Buckland   *Logbook of a fisherman and
zoologist*, 1876

It never remained above ground any longer than it took to
devour its prey [earthworms]; after this it sank into the earth
as a submarine sinks into the water.

Konrad Lorenz   *King Solomon's ring*, 1952

The mole goes down the slow dark personal passage –
a haberdasher's sample of wet velvet moving
on fine feet through an earth that only
the gardener and the excavator know.

Patricia K. Page   *The mole*, 1947

Scarce disappears the deluge, when the mole,
Close prisoner long in subterranean cell
Frost-bound, again the miner plays, and heaves,
With treble industry, the mellow mound
Along the swarded vale.

James Hurdis   *The village curate*, 1788

An intelligent-looking shepherd told me that he had been
shepherding on these hills above forty years, and the moles
had always been there where they had no water to drink.
'They must drink or die,' said I; 'it is down in the books, and
therefore it must be true.' He shook his head at the books and

replied that the moles come out at night to lick the grass – the dew was enough for them.

W. H. Hudson   *Nature in downland*, 1923

The dead leaves at the bottom of the ditch heave up as if something was pushing underneath; and after a while, as he comes to the heap of sand thrown out by the rabbits, a mole emerges, and instantly, with a shiver, throws off the particles of dust upon his fur as a dog fresh from the water sends a shower from his coat.

Richard Jefferies   *The gamekeeper at home*, 1878

He scrooged and scrabbled and scratched and scraped, working busily with his little paws and muttering to himself, 'Up we go! Up we go!' till at last, pop! his snout came out into the sunlight.

Kenneth Grahame   *The wind in the willows*, 1908

Pray you, tread softly, that the blind mole may not
Hear a foot fall: we now are near his cell.

William Shakespeare   *The tempest*, 1611

The eyes of moles and of some burrowing rodents are rudimentary in size, and in some cases are quite covered by skin and fur.

Charles Darwin   *On the origin of species*, 1859

That moles have eyes in their head, is manifest unto any(one) that wants them not in his own.

Thomas Browne   *Vulgar errors*, 1646

Mongoose

Out slipped a beautiful reddish-brown creature, thin and lithe, with the legs of a stoat, a long thin nose, and a pair of the finest red eyes that I ever saw in an animal's head. 'It's a mongoose!' I cried.

A. Conan Doyle   *The crooked man*, 1893

He was a mongoose, rather like a little cat in his fur and his tail, but quite like a weasel in his head and his habits. His eyes and the end of his restless nose were pink; he could scratch himself anywhere he pleased with any leg.

Rudyard Kipling   *Rikki-Tikki-Tavi*, 1894

When excited, the mongoose erects its long stiff hair, and it must be very difficult for a snake to drive its fangs through this and through the thick skin.

W. T. Blanford quoted in *Harmsworth natural history*, 1910

Mongooses provided Elsa [the lion cub] with a lot of fun. These little creatures, no bigger than a weasel, live in abandoned termite hills, made of cement-hard soil . . . and built with many air funnels . . . Elsa would sit absolutely still in front of the ant-hill, besieging them, apparently deriving great satisfaction from seeing the little clowns popping their heads out of the air funnels.

Joy Adamson *Born free*, 1960

Monkey

MAN AND MONKEY

In a few passages [of Shakespeare's plays] there seems to be some sort of implication that the monkey is simply a degraded form of man.

C. T. Onions in *Shakespeare's England*, 1916

The strain of man's bred out
Into baboon and monkey. (*Apemantus*, a churlish philosopher)

William Shakespeare *Timon of Athens, c.* 1607

I could never look long upon a Monkey, without very Mortifying Reflections.

William Congreve *Letter to Mr Dennis*, 1695

MONKEYS ON THE MOVE

The monkeys walk together
Holding their neighbours' tails.

Rudyard Kipling *The legends of evil*, 1892

You will never see an Old World monkey hanging from a branch by its tail while it uses all four limbs to gather its food. This is just one of the many differences between Old World and New World monkeys.

Rosamund Fisher *My jungle babies*, 1979

The small monkeys capering on the boughs.

James Montgomery   *The pelican island*, 1828

Monkeys darted away, some to the tree-tops, where they sat alert and ready to swing from branch to branch.

Cherry Kearton   *The animals came to drink*, 1932

Where a pack of monkeys had travelled over the road, the smell of them lingered for a long time in the air, a dry and stale, mousy smell.

Karen Blixen   *Out of Africa*, 1937

SKIN SCRUTINY

In spite of an almost universal belief, monkeys are extremely rarely infested with fleas . . . In most cases, a monkey searching another monkey is not hunting for fleas but for little masses of salt-tasting secretion.

P. Chalmers Mitchell   *Guide to the London zoo*

Healthy wild monkeys are much too clean and active to harbour fleas.

Harold Russell   *The flea*, 1913

MONKEY ACTIVITY

[For monkeys] cars are free rides, chariots to play with, containers for bigger apes who might foolishly lower the windows and be relieved of their goodies, and bearers of bright, shiny bits of detachable material (screen-wipers, wing mirrors, radio aerials, and the like) which can be taken away for trophies.

David Taylor   *Next panda, please*, 1982

It must of course be taken into account that monkeys, in their physical execution of whatever they are mentally equipped to do, are greatly helped by their man-like hands.

Ludwig Heck   *Bobby the chimpanzee and other friends*, 1931

On board the steamer were two common monkeys from India. The smaller monkey one day fell overboard. The larger one became frantically excited and, running to the side, held on by one hand, leaned over and, with the other hand, extended to the monkey in the water the cord by which the would-be rescuer was tied at the waist.

Ernest A. Bryant   in *Harmsworth natural history*, 1910

[It is believed] that Malayan jungle monkeys have a well-established and widely recognized language, for themselves and for other animals – a language which clearly distinguishes between animals and reptiles that are dangerous and the ones that are not.

Ronald McKie   *The company of animals*, 1965

BABOONS

It seems a fact that baboons have a language of their own, and that in danger the old animals give their commands by means of some simple method of speech.

C. G. Schilling   *With flashlight and rifle*, 1906

The watchful old baboon saw a glint of brownish yellow [cheetah] move behind a bush, and he called out – the quick bark with which baboons tell of urgent danger . . . The clamour of shouting baboons continued for several minutes. Then the leader of the troop gave the shout which means 'All clear'.

Cherry Kearton   *The animals came to drink*, 1932

The Big Baboon who lives upon
The plains of Caribou,
He goes about with nothing on –
A shocking thing to do.

Hilaire Belloc   *The bad child's book of beasts*, 1896

In Egypt oft has seen the sot bow down
And reverence some deified baboon.

John Oldham   *Poems and translations*, 1683

The ancient Egyptians apparently tamed the baboon and [tried to] train it to ascend palm trees and throw down the fruit. But there is silence in research as to the final results of this experiment.

H. H. Johnston   *The taming of the wild*, 1910

One of the big baboons, having good cause to suspect his wife of infidelity, drowned her in the bathing-pool, and over her dead body challenged his rival.

    Helen M. Sidebotham   *Mysteries of the zoo*, 1927

I heard the inquiring bark of a baboon peeping through the foliage; then the bush became alive with inquisitive watching faces. Soon they came more and more into the open . . . One little chap fell with a splash into the river. At once an old baboon came to its rescue, and clutching the wet, struggling creature, rushed off with it to safety.

    Joy Adamson   *Born free*, 1960

Baboons are very greedy after emmets [ants]. Having found an emmet hill, they presently surround it, and, laying their forepaws upon the ant-heap, as fast as the emmets creep into their treacherous palms, they lick them off with great comfort to their stomachs.

    Job Ludolf   *History of Ethiopia*, 1684

Okapi

The Okapi, which looks as though it hadn't been able to make up its mind whether it wanted to be a zebra or a giraffe, has an incredible turn of speed and the characteristic of leaping high into the air every few paces.

    Colin Howard   in *Evening News*, 28 Aug. 1948

Opossum

When there is no apparent escape from danger, the animal sinks into a state of complete nervous paralysis that can last for just a few minutes or several hours, in the hope that the danger will just go away . . . The device relies heavily on the animal being attacked only by predators that turn up their noses at carrion – dead animals that they have not despatched themselves.

    Joyce Everett   in *RSPCA Today*, spring, 1983

Otter

Beautiful, rare, and secretive – the otter is one of our most delightful animals, yet one of the most elusive.

Radio Times, 24 Dec. 1982

The most beautiful and engaging of all elegant pets. There seems no end to its fun, its energy, its drollery, its good nature, and its postures of new and surprising grace.

Ernest Thompson Seton *Life histories of northern animals*, 1910

The otter is an ornament to the river [Thames], and is more worthy of preservation than any other creature.

Richard Jefferies *The open air*, 1885

On the whole, animals and men would get along together much better apart – particularly the last seventy otters left in England.

Mike Harding *The armchair anarchist's almanac*, 1981

Tarka was awakened by the tremendous baying of hounds. He saw feet splashing in the shallow water, a row of noses . . . He crouched a yard away, against the cold rock. The noise hurt the fine drums of his ears. Hob-nailed boots scraped on the brown shillets of the water-bed, and iron-tipped hunting poles tapped the rocks.

Henry Williamson *Tarka the otter*, 1927

The eldest and biggest of the litter was a dog-cub, and when he first drew breath he was less than five inches long.

Henry Williamson *Tarka the otter*, 1927

They heard their mother's whistle. The cry was not as piercing as the dog otter's call to his mate, but like wet fingers drawn down a pane of glass.

Henry Williamson *Tarka the otter*, 1927

She opened her mouth and panted, which is the way otters laugh among themselves.

Henry Williamson *Tarka the otter*, 1927

I saw that Mij was floating on his back, apparently fast asleep, with a bunch of scarlet rowan berries clasped to his chest with one arm. Such bright objects as this he would often pick up on his walks.

   Gavin Maxwell   *Ring of bright water*, 1960

At the end of its meal the sea otter licks its 'fingers' to get the last of the taste, and then washes vigorously. It rolls over and over. It scrubs the fur tablecloth of its chest and stomach. It rubs its forepaws together like a man using soap and water. It washes its face, even going behind its tiny ears.

   Edwin Way Teale   *Autumn across America*, 1956

Panther

Black panthers are simply leopards that happen to have very dark brown hair.

   Michael Boorer   *Wild cats*, 1969

We heard tell of the strange nature of one of the beasts, that he holds his domain amid the mountain caves. That beast is called Panther . . . When he receives food, he seeks rest after the feasting.

   Physiologus (Anglo-Saxon)

Sleeping in beauty on their mangled prey,
As panthers sleep.

   P. B. Shelley   *Letter to Maria Gisborne*, 1820

He was a lovely Youth! I guess
The panther in the wilderness
Was not so fair as he.

   William Wordsworth   *Ruth*, 1800

Is any Panther's rage
So furious, any torrent's fall so swift
As a wrong'd woman's hate?

   Nathaniel Lee   *The rival queens*, 1677

Porcupine

[Make] each particular hair to stand on end,
Like quills upon the fretful porcupine.

   William Shakespeare   *Hamlet*, 1604

The BARD & his Porcupine.

The porcupine baby, almost alone among the babes of the wild, was exempted, through the reputation of his spines, from the law of silence as the price of life. Young or old, the porcupine will make a noise whenever it pleases him to do so.

C. G. D. Roberts *Some animal stories*, 1920

If attacked by dogs or other four-footed foes, porcupines rush backwards and inflict severe wounds with the long quills on their hind quarters.

Harmsworth natural history, 1910

The porcupine rolled itself into a ball, radiating long, sharp needles in all directions that defied attack. In his youth One Eye [an old wolf] had once sniffed too near a similar, apparently inert ball of quills, and had the tail flick out suddenly in his face. One quill he had carried away in his muzzle, where it had remained for weeks.

Jack London *White Fang*, 1905

Puma (Cougar)

Pumas are seen relatively rarely. This is because they are cautious and shy, and are most often active at night.

Michael Boorer *Wild cats*, 1969

In North America the puma is generally known as the mountain lion.

Harmsworth natural history, 1910

There are stories that mountain lions have tried to make friends with people by approaching them with the playful attitude of kittens.

Osmond P. Breland *Animal friends and foes*, 1958

On presenting it [a puma] with an orange or any other thing, it handled it with its forepaws, playing with it in the same way as a cat does with a mouse . . . When rubbed or tickled it lay down and purred like a cat.

Felix D'Azara *Natural history of Paraguay*, 1801
[This puma had been tamed by a village priest.]

At night a traveller made his bed under the shelter of a rock . . . About nine in the evening four pumas appeared . . . After

a while they began to gambol together close to him,
concealing themselves from each other among the rocks, just
as kittens do, and frequently while pursuing one another
leaping over him.

W. H. Hudson *The naturalist in La Plata*, 1892

What is he carrying?
Something yellow.
A deer? . . .
It is a mountain lion,
A long, long slim cat, yellow like a lioness,
Dead.
He trapped her this morning, he says, smiling foolishly . . .
What a gap in the world, the missing white frost-face
of that slim yellow mountain lion.

D. H. Lawrence *Collected poems*, 1922

There are numerous reports to the effect that even a cornered
South American cougar does not defend itself from man but
simply resigns itself to its fate.

Osmond P. Breland *Animal friends and foes*, 1958

The early Spanish-American naturalists attributed the fact
that the puma would not attack man or child, nor defend
itself against a man's attack, to extreme 'timidity' or
'cowardice'. It was a false description of an animal noted for
its ferocity towards all other beasts.

W. H. Hudson in *Harmsworth natural history*,
1910

A Spanish girl who was tied to a tree by a Spanish Governor
for visiting the Indians avowed that a puma had sat by her all
night, and driven the other beasts away. This was regarded as
a miracle, but it would not now excite surprise.

C. J. Cornish *Animals today*, 1898

Rabbit

I love to peep out on a summer's morn
Just as the scouting rabbit seeks her shed.

John Clare *Summer morning*, 1821

The rabbit fondles his own harmless face.

Alfred Tennyson *Aylmer's field*, 1864

MUNCH, MUNCH, MUNCH!

There is the stench of those munching, lop-eared rabbits that
now inhabit a part of the stable, but then on the other hand
they do consume about two hundred dandelions a day, and
dandelions are one of our noxious weeds.

C. C. Vyvyan *A Cornish year, 1959*

The dry slope was dotted with rabbits – some nibbling at the
thin grass near their holes, others pushing farther down to
look for dandelions.

Richard Adams *Watership Down, 1972*

When the wild rabbit first goes forth to graze in the late
afternoon it eats voraciously, nibbling down grass and
vegetation in scythe-like movements of the jaws from one
side to another, raising the head at intervals to look around.

R. M. Lockley *The private life of the rabbit, 1965*

BURROWS AND BARROWS

A specially enlarged entrance may be found somewhere in
most of the banks frequented by rabbits . . . It may be a kind
of ancestral hall, the favourite cave of the first (rodent)
settlers here, clung to by their descendants.

Richard Jefferies *Wild life in a southern county, 1879*

It is a curious fact that rabbits are often to be found
inhabiting burrows which hold badgers, but it should be
added that the rabbits use only those passages which are too
small for their enemies to get through.

George A. B. Dewar *Wild life in Hampshire
highlands, 1899*

Sometimes a bunny will appear at the mouth of a hole which
your knee nearly touches. He stops dead, as if petrified with
astonishment, sitting on his haunches. His full dark eye is on
you with a gaze of intense curiosity.

Richard Jefferies *The gamekeeper at home, 1878*

When I first set eyes on those acres [near Hambledon,
Surrey] they were brown with rabbits. So was the side of the
lane brown with their burrows.

Eric Parker *Surrey, 1947*

The rabbit is an active agent in demolishing the barrows and other earthworks. He burrows into the mound and throws out bushels of chalk and clay, which is soon washed down by the rains; he tunnels it through and through.

   W. H. Hudson   *A shepherd's life*, 1910

One afternoon when walking on Bishop Down I noticed that a rabbit . . . had thrown out a human thigh-bone and a rib or two . . . The following day I went again and there were more bones, and every day after that the number increased.

   W. H. Hudson   *A shepherd's life*, 1910

Winter snow fell and became a few inches thick . . . Yet rabbits only occasionally scratch away the snow, and so get at the grass, though the natural instinct of rabbits is to dig.

   Richard Jefferies   *Wild life in a southern county*, 1879

Buck rabbits on their own seldom or never go in for serious digging. This is the natural job of a doe making a home for her litter before they are born, and then her buck helps her.

   Richard Adams   *Watership Down*, 1972

GUN AND TRAP

Nature never did a crueller thing than when she gave rabbits white tails: it makes it possible to shoot them long after it is too dark to see any other quarry.

   E. V. Lucas   *Harvest home*, 1913

At Maesllwch Castle last week four guns killed seven hundred rabbits in one afternoon.

   Francis Kilvert   *Diary*, 1870

I hear a sudden cry of pain!
There is a rabbit in a snare:
Now I hear the cry again,
But I cannot tell from where . . .
Little one! Oh, little one!
I am searching everywhere!

   James Stephens   *The snare*, 1915

Lying in an iron trap
He cries all through the deafened night –

Until his smiling murderer comes
To kill him in the morning light.
  W. H. Davies *The rabbit*, 1941

A baby rabbit
With eyes full of pus
Is the work of scientific us.
  Spike Milligan *Myxomatosis*, 1972

RABBIT MAGIC

It was bringing radiance into my friend's life to know that his
old hat, which had done nothing more romantic than keep his
head warm all these years, was . . . to be used for magical
purposes, and have a real rabbit extracted from it.
  E. V. Lucas *Character and comedy*, 1907

The production of a rabbit from a top hat is sometimes used
to symbolize magic, although it is not an old trick, a good one,
or one frequently performed.
  Geoffrey Lamb *Magic illustrated dictionary*, 1979

Sir David Wilkie's celebrated *The Rabbit on the Wall* [was]
completed in 1816 and exhibited at the Royal Academy that
year . . . A candle-lit cottage interior shows the father
producing a rabbit shadow on the wall, to the obvious delight
of the four children.
  Edwin A. Dawes *The great illusionists*, 1979

It was estimated some years ago that . . . about ten million
rabbits' feet were sold in the U.S.A. annually.
  Douglas Hill *Magic and superstition*, 1968
  [A rabbit's foot is supposed by the credulous to ward off bad
luck.]

RABBIT RASCALITY

The rabbit has a charming face;
Its private life is a disgrace:
I really dare not name to you
The awful things that rabbits do.
  Anon. quoted in *Faber book of comic verse*, 1942

The rabbits in the embankment of the old Midhurst to Petworth railway have been digging up the hallowed Amersham polo ground.

James Preston   in *Daily Telegraph*, 22 Aug. 1983

Rat

A MULTIPLICITY OF RATS

Out of the houses the rats came tumbling.
Great rats, small rats, lean rats, brawny rats,
Brown rats, black rats, grey rats, tawny rats.

Robert Browning   *The pied piper of Hamelin*, 1845

The Zoo, like the town of Hamelin, is infested with rats, and when the houses are comparatively free from visitors these rodents are in every corner collecting food that has fallen out of the cages.

Helen M. Sidebotham   *Mysteries of the zoo*, 1927

Nothing could keep down the multiplicity of rats on board the *Advance*, their impudence increasing with their numbers. At last they were everywhere, under the stove, in the steward's lockers, in the cushions, about the beds. A mother rat bit Kane's finger to the bone one day as he was pushing his hand into a bearskin mitten which she had selected for her nest.

The exploring voyages of Dr Kane, 1860
[Kane's Arctic voyage was made in 1853–5.]

'I've often seed as many as a hundred rats at once, and they're woppers in the sewers, I can tell you. Them there water-rats, too, is far more ferociouser than any other rats, and they'd think nothing of tackling a man.'

Henry Mayhew   *London labour and the London poor*, 1861
[Quoting a sewer-walker.]

And in at the windows and in at the door,
And through the walls helter-skelter they pour,
And down from the ceiling and up through the floor,
From the right and the left, from behind and before . . .
They have whetted their teeth against the stones.

  Robert Southey *God's judgment on a wicked bishop*, 1799

Though trapped, shot, and ferretted without mercy, the rats insist on a share of the good things going. They specially haunt the pigsties, and when the pigs are served with their food, they feed with them at the same trough.

  Richard Jefferies *Wild life in a southern county*, 1879

TROUBLED WITH A RAT

What if my house be troubled with a rat
And I be pleased to give ten thousand ducats
To have it baned?

  William Shakespeare *The merchant of Venice*, c. 1596

In my college rooms at Christchurch a bachelor rat had taken up his quarters. The scout used to put out breakfast before chapel, and when I returned I frequently found marks of the rat's paws and teeth on the butter pats.

  Frank Buckland *Curiosities of natural history*, 1857

A rat's private life, a rat's thoughts and conversation, may be far more wholesome than a rabbit's. Yet a thousand rabbits might play on the floor of my bedroom all night, and be hanged to them, while if a single rat so much as scratched beneath the flooring I would lose all sleep.

  E. V. Lucas *Harvest home*, 1913

RAT DESERTION

A rotten carcase of a boat . . . The very rats
Instinctively have quit it.

  William Shakespeare *The tempest*, 1611

Sailors almost everywhere believe that if all the rats suddenly desert a ship just before she sails, that ship is doomed.

Although rats are not now as common on board ship as they used to be, the tradition persists.

E. & M. A. Radford   *Encyclopedia of superstitions*, 1948

It is the wisdom of rats, that will be sure to leave a house somewhat before it falls.

Francis Bacon   *Of wisdom for a man's self*, 1625

Reindeer

It is upon the reindeer that the Laplander is dependent for (almost) every comfort in life. The reindeer is his estate, his horse, his cow, his companion, and his friend.

Lord Dufferin   *Letters from high latitudes*, 1859

Their reindeer form their riches. These their tents,
Their robes, their beds, and all their homely wealth . . .
Obsequious at their call, the docile tribe
Yield to the sled their necks, and whirl them swift
O'er hill and dale, heaped into one expanse
Of marbled snow, as far as eye can reach.

James Thomson   *The seasons, winter*, 1726

As soon as a young lady is born, she is dowered by her father with a certain number of reindeer, which are immediately branded with her initials, and thenceforth kept apart as her especial property.

Lord Dufferin   *Letters from high latitudes*, 1859

He stood on a hill in the middle of the passing throng with a clear view of ten miles each way and it was one army of caribou [reindeer].

Ottawa Naturalist, 1917

Jack went on the Barrens [Canadian North-West] to look for Caribou but saw nothing. (1927)

Edgar Christian   *Unflinching*, 1937
[Christian, aged 18, and his two companions died of starvation in 1927. Diary found *two* years later.]

Rhinoceros

You have a horn where other beasts have none:
Rhinoceros, you are an ugly beast.

    Hilaire Belloc   *Bad child's book of beasts*, 1896

The rhinoceros has a good sense of smell and hears well, but
its eyesight is supposedly on a par with that of a near-sighted
man who has lost his spectacles.

    Osmond P. Breland   *Animal friends and foes*, 1958

They are a belligerent lot and will charge a truck often
enough for its occupants to plan a fast exit route whenever
they see a rhino lurch into view.

    Anthony Smith   *Throw out two hands*, 1963

The black species . . . is the most unpredictable of African
animals. Occasionally it will charge a car, and nearly always it
will go for a man on foot if he approaches too close. With over
a ton weight coming at you at twenty miles an hour you don't
stand much of a chance.

    Alan Moorehead   *No room in the ark*, 1959

I learned that many will run away at the first suggestion of
man, but that some will hesitate, and retire three paces, and
hesitate and advance three paces, and hesitate again. Just
occasionally one will come for you in a blundering rush.

    K. Gandar Dower   *The spotted lion*, 1937

Badak [rhinoceros] is a creature of routine . . . He uses the
same game trails and, as he likes to bathe in mud, he goes
with dangerous regularity to his favourite wallow and lies up
to his ears during the hot part of the day.

    Ronald McKie   *The company of animals*, 1965

They drank first, and then lay rolling and wallowing in the
mud at the edge of the water, till a dampish reddish covering
was smeared over the greater part of their bodies. Then . . .
they began to play. Heavily, lumberingly, they chased one
another round and round the little pool.

    Cherry Kearton   *The animals came to drink*, 1932

Rhino are being poached out of existence, and within ten
years at most the black rhino will have ceased to exist. Arabs

in the North Yemen will now pay up to £5000 for the handle
of a dagger if it is made of rhino horn.

David Shepherd (wildlife artist) quoted in
Hampshire Chronicle, 23 Dec. 1983

I once saw a white rhinoceros give a buffalo which was gazing
intently at myself a poke in the chest, but it did not wound it,
and seemed only a hint to get out of the way.

David Livingstone *Travels in South Africa*, 1857

Seal

When the islands frequented by these seals were first visited
by voyagers the poor animals had not the slightest fear of
man. They would lie quite still while their comrades were
knocked on the head and skinned. But in a few years they
became intimidated, and placed themselves on rocks from
which they could immediately dive into the sea.

James Weddell *Voyage towards the South Pole*, 1825

I meet my mates in the morning, a broken scattered band.
Men shoot us in the water and club us on the land.

Rudyard Kipling *Lukannon*, 1894

Men can walk among the drowsy giants – they weigh in the
neighbourhood of five hundred pounds – with complete
impunity. The animals merely raise their heads, sometimes
growl a little, and fall back to sleep. (Weddell seal)

Thomas R. Henry *The white continent*, 1951

The mother pushes her child into the water to make it learn
to swim. One observer watched a pup figuratively stick its toe
in the icy water and shudder, whereupon the mother rose out
of the water, seized it by the scruff of the neck, and pulled it
in.

Walter Sullivan *Quest for a continent*, 1957

We camped that night close to a seal hole. We were somewhat
disturbed that night by the snorting and whistling of the seals
as they came up for their blows.

Ernest Shackleton *The heart of the Antarctic*, 1909

Our vertical position seemed to puzzle them. Becoming aware of our presence, they would stare at us in blank amazement with their great soft eyes, and roll over and regard us sideways, first on one side, then on the other; then they would lie on their backs and scrutinize us upside-down, in the vain endeavour to see us horizontally and make us into seals.

H. G. Ponting *The great white south*, 1921

Tales are told of seals which have become so thoroughly tame that they will come and lie before the fire, making friends with the dog and cat. (Canadian seal)

Wilfred Grenfell *Vikings of today*, 1895

The Eskimos about Bering Strait believe that the souls of dead sea-beasts, such as seals . . . remain attached to their bladders, and that by returning the bladders to the sea they can cause the souls to be reincarnated in fresh bodies and so multiply the game which the hunters pursue and kill.

James G. Frazer *The golden bough*, 1922

Sea-leopard

We soon became acquainted with the sea-leopard, which waits under the ice-foot for the little penguins; he is a brute, but sinuous and graceful.

Apsley Cherry-Garrard *The worst journey in the world*, 1922

The sea leopard is the most predacious of the seal family . . . It will attack a man without provocation and probably could slash off a leg or arm with its long, curved teeth.

Thomas R. Henry *The white continent*, 1951

What in the darkness I had taken for a complacent Weddell seal was really a very different kind of beast . . . with array of teeth that it showed in a most aggressive manner. Day shouted to me: 'Look out! It's a Sea-leopard! It'll bite your leg off!' I did look out; and I put up the smartest bit of dodging and sprinting, with the beast wriggling and flapping after me, close at my heels.

H. G. Ponting *The great white south*, 1921

Sea-lion

Each herd of sea-lions was observed to place some of their
males at a distance, in the nature of sentinels . . . and they
were capable of alarming even at a considerable distance, for
the noise they make is very loud, and of different kinds,
sometimes grunting like hogs, and at other times snorting
like horses in full vigour.

   George Anson   *Voyage round the world*, 1748

Shrew

There was a small animal running about the stones by the
brookside in the sun . . . sometimes almost on its side,
showing its white belly, tumbling about, darting to and fro
rapidly, and conducting itself in the most earnest but
ludicrous manner.

   Francis Kilvert   *Diary*, 1870

Like penguins, the water-shrews looked rather awkward and
ungainly on dry land but were transformed into objects of
elegance and grace on entering the water . . . Under water the
protruding belly balanced harmoniously the curve of their
back and gave a beautifully symmetrical streamline.

   Konrad Lorenz   *King Solomon's ring*, 1952

It was supposed [by the superstitious] that the shrewmouse is
of so baneful and deleterious a nature, that wherever it creeps
over a beast, be it horse, cow, or sheep, the suffering animal is
afflicted with cruel anguish.

   Gilbert White   *Natural history of Selborne*, 1776

Strange to say, Shakespeare has no allusion to the
shrewmouse, whose supposed evil influence on cattle had
been for centuries a favourite subject of allusion, and may
well have been the origin of the application of the word
'shrew' to human beings of ill-grained disposition.

   C. T. Onions   in *Shakespeare's England*, 1916

Skunk

One biologist has said that skunks are the most important
mammalian enemies of insects, and another, even more
enthusiastic, has stated that skunks destroy more insects than
all other mammals combined.

    Osmond P. Breland   *Animal friends and foes*, 1958

I learnt from my old cook that if one gets up and rides out
into the camp at sunrise one will see the meeting of the
skunks. I rode out to see this one morning early and sure
enough I saw a fascinating sight, about twelve of them sitting
in a horseshoe, with one old chap at the head. (South
America)

    Barbara Woodhouse   *Talking to animals*, 1954

The secretion that has given the skunk such an ill name is
contained in a pair of glands situated beneath the tail, and can
be ejected at the will of the animal. So forcibly can the fluid
be ejected that it will carry a distance of thirteen to a little
over sixteen feet.

    Harmsworth natural history, 1910

Sloth

The sloth, about the size of a large sheepdog, hung upside
down and stared at me with an expression of ineffable sadness
on its furry face. Slowly it opened its mouth, exposing its
black enamel-less teeth, and did its best to frighten me by
making the loudest noise of which it is capable – a faint
bronchial wheeze.

    David Attenborough   *Zoo quest to Guyana*, 1956

In moving-slow he has no peer.
You ask him something in his ear;
He thinks about it for a year.

    Theodore Roethke   *The sloth*, 1957

Squirrel

To me, squirrels are almost fairy people. They are
marvellously round: roundly curved body, curved shell-like

ears, curved haunches, tail either S-curved over the back like a mantle, or flying straight out behind the long slender body.

Joan Ward-Harris *Creature comforts*, 1979

On a cold windy day the squirrel lays its tail along its back and hunches under it as though to keep warm.

Monica Shorten *Squirrels*, 1954

As peacocks cover themselves with their tails in hot summer, from the rage of the sun as under a shadow, with the same disposition doth the squirrel cover her body against hot or cold.

Edward Topsell *The historie of foure-footed beastes*, 1607

RED AND GREY

Usually the red squirrel waked me up in the dawn, coursing over the roof.

H. D. Thoreau *Walden*, 1854

This alien species [grey squirrel] was first introduced to England in the parks of Bournemouth.

Ralph Whitlock *Wildlife in Wessex*, 1976

With the spread of the grey squirrel across England and Wales this century, and the fruitless campaign to control it, there has arisen a popular belief that grey squirrels are pests but that red squirrels are harmless. So it comes as a surprise to many to be told that thousands of red squirrels have in the past been slaughtered as pests, especially in Scotland.

William Condry *Woodlands*, 1974

I sometimes have grey squirrels in my garden, but my enjoyment of them has been spoiled by constant reminders that they are pests. The other day *The Daily Telegraph* informed me that the grey squirrel is the only serious enemy of the minute wasp that is threatening Britain's oak trees, so perhaps now I may enjoy my squirrels with an easy conscience.

Mary Furneaux letter in *Daily Telegraph*, 18 Oct. 1983

SQUIRREL ACTIVITY

He sees me, and at once, swift as a bird,
Ascends the neighb'ring beech; there whisks his brush,
And perks his ears, and stamps and scolds aloud,
With all the prettiness of feigned alarm.

  William Cowper *The task*, 1785

He skips
Along the highest branches, along
Tree-fingers slender as string,
Fur tail following, to the very tips.

  Ian Serraillier *The squirrel*, 1963

When alarmed or chased, a squirrel always ascends the tree
on the opposite side from you: he will not run to a solitary
tree if he can possibly avoid it; he likes a group, and his trick
is, the moment he thinks he is out of sight among the upper
branches, to slip quietly from one tree to the other till, while
you are scanning every bough, he has travelled fifty yards
away unnoticed.

  Richard Jefferies *Wild life in a southern county*,
1879

Squirrels are as voluble as fishwives. If you would test the
squirrel's powers of repartee, you must drive one to the
branches of an isolated tree and then rap the trunk with a
stick.

  E. V. Lucas *Harvest home*, 1913

There is something very human in the apparent mirth and
mockery of squirrels. It seems to be a sort of ironical
laughter. 'What a ridiculous thing you are, to be sure!' he
seems to say; 'how clumsy and awkward, and what a poor
show for a tail!'

  John Burroughs *The snow-walkers*, 1893

All day long the squirrels came and went. One would
approach at first warily through the shrub-oaks, running over
the snow crust by fits and starts like a leaf blown by the wind
. . . then suddenly pausing with a ludicrous expression and a
gratuitous somersault.

  H. D. Thoreau *Walden*, 1854

The smallest squirrel reached my jacket cuff after several minutes of circumspect stalking. The cuff didn't seem dangerous, so the intrepid little explorer climbed up my sleeve, watching ahead and around.

Helen Hoover *A place in the woods*, 1970

I watched with much interest and amusement a red squirrel extracting fallen chestnuts from their prickly cases and burying them one after another in the lawn. It scratched, made a little hole, carefully pushed the nut into it, and then, using its long-fingered forepaws like hands, even more carefully covered it up.

Frances Pitt *Meet us in the garden*, 1946

Against winter it was well prepared
With many a store in hollow root or tree,
As if being told what winter's wants would be.

John Clare *The village minstrel*, 1821

Once or twice I offered a couple of nuts that I knew from their weight to be empty, and these crafty little beggars wasted no time. They just dropped each one without attempting to crack it. Then they gave me a look which plainly said, 'Who d'you think you're trying to fool?'

Percy Edwards *Percy Edwards' country book*, 1980

Stoat

Stoats, though not as numerous as weasels, probably do quite as much injury, being larger, swifter, stronger, and very bold, sometimes entering sheds close to dwelling-houses. The labouring elder folk declare that they have been known to suck the blood of infants left asleep in a cradle on the floor, biting the child behind the ear.

Richard Jefferies *The gamekeeper at home*, 1878

The rabbit's appearance when he is being pursued by a stoat, his trembling frame, little hopping movements, and agonising cries, remind us of our own state in a bad dream . . . when we must put forth our utmost speed to escape instant destruction, yet have a leaden weight on our limbs.

W. H. Hudson *Hampshire days*, 1903

Saw a stoat run into a hole in the garden wall; went up to it
and endeavoured to lure the little beast out by mimicking a
rat's or Mouse's squeak . . . Succeeded, to my astonishment.
He came half out of the hole and looked in my face.

J. E. Millais   *Diary*, 1851

Tiger

FIERCE AND LONELY

Tiger! Tiger! burning bright
In the forests of the night,
What immortal hand or eye
Dare frame thy fearful symmetry?

William Blake   *Songs of experience*, 1794

The nocturnal terror in gold,
Red-fire coated, green-fire-eyed,
The fanged, the clawed, the frightful leaper,
Great-sinewed, silent walker.

Ruth Pitter   *The tigress*

Rimau is the jungle's loneliest animal. All his fellows dislike
him, from the largest, the elephant, to the smallest, the
mousedeer, though this dislike is tempered with respect . . .
Rimau never loses his pride, his independent spirit, his
aldermanic dignity.

Ronald McKie   *The company of animals*, 1965
[Rimau is the Malayan term for tiger.]

Tigers, of course, have solitary habits
And haunt where brown and yellow leaves are strown;
They're not companionable beasts like rabbits
And much prefer to eat their meals alone.

W. C. Smith   *Moral-sublime*, 1891

I was suddenly startled by an unpleasantly malevolent snarl.
Looking to the left, I could clearly distinguish between the
matted undergrowth the form of a large tiger, not more than
five yards away. Apart from zoos and circuses, it was the first
time I had ever seen a tiger.

F. S. Smythe   *The Kanchenjunga adventure*, 1931
[The 'malevolent' snarl was more probably a startled one.
The tiger made no attack.]

When the blast of war blows in our ears
Then imitate the action of the tiger;
Stiffen the sinews, summon up the blood,
Disguise fair nature with ill-favour'd rage.

  William Shakespeare *Henry V*, 1599

The tiger's usual attack is a rush, accompanied by a series of short, deep growls, or roars, in which he evidently thinks he will do much by intimidation.

  Joseph Fayrer *The royal tiger of Bengal*, 1875

TIGER-HUNTING

Dined . . . with Captain Hill, a tall handsome powerful man who, when tiger hunting once in India, was seized by a tiger at the back of his neck. But he so pommelled the tiger's face over his shoulder that the beast let go, leaving Captain Hill, however, with a stiff neck for life.

  Francis Kilvert *Diary*, 1873

The Koreans hunt the tiger during one half of the year, while the tiger hunts the Koreans during the other half.

  Old Chinese saying

O I love to hunt the tiger bold
With shouting loud and free,
In jungles where the sands of gold
Border the black Gangee.

But when the tiger turns about
And takes to hunting me,
That's not so fine – I'd rather shout
As hunter than huntee.

  Ambrose Bierce *The enlarged devil's dictionary*, 1967

TIGER'S CALL

The tiger's usual call is very similar to that of a lion – a prolonged moaning, thrilling sound, repeated twice or thrice, becoming louder and quicker.

  W. T. Blanford *The fauna of British India*, 1888–91

To my dismay Tiger-Price suddenly gave vent to a hoarse roar that concluded with a muffled and yearning purring – that, he explained, was the call of the female tiger on heat – and to my consternation two or three gentlemen tigers appeared to be interested in her offer and set up a cheerful roaring from different points of the jungle.

Olle Strandberg   *Tigerland and south sea*, 1953

LONG LIVE THE TIGER!

In India Hindoos especially hold the tiger in superstitious awe: many would not kill him if they could, nor are they always willing to show where he may be found, even when he has been killing their comrades or their cattle, from the fear that he may haunt them, or do them mischief, after he is dead.

Joseph Fayrer   in *Nineteenth century*, 1889

I don't *want* the tiger superseded . . . May each one eat at least seventy miserable featherless human birds, and lick red chops of gusto after it.

D. H. Lawrence   *Selected letters*

It seems to me the tiger
Has not been lately fed,
Not for a day or two at least,
And that is why the noble beast
Has bitten off your head.

A. E. Housman   *Light verse and parodies* in *A.E.H.*,
ed. Laurence Housman, 1937

A tiger is striped and golden for his own glory.

D. H. Lawrence   *Self-protection*, 1929

The author who first used the words 'as cruel as a tiger' and 'bloodthirsty as a tiger' . . . showed a lamentable ignorance of the animal he defamed.

Jim Corbett   *The man-eaters of Kumaon*, 1946

The tiger is a large-hearted gentleman with boundless courage.

Jim Corbett   *The man-eaters of Kumaon*, 1946

Vole

A quantity of sap had oozed out of a large elm tree, and a hornet had discovered it . . . Stealing up to the lower end of the sap a vole, too, began feeding on it. The hornet, who was at the upper end, at once stopped eating and regarded the intruder for some time, then advanced towards him in a threatening attitude . . . The vole slipped quietly down and hid himself at the roots.

    W. H. Hudson   *Hampshire days*, 1903

Walrus

'The time has come,' the Walrus said,
'To talk of many things.'

    Lewis Carroll   *Through the looking-glass*, 1871

The walruses were here [off Spitzbergen] very numerous, lying in herds upon the ice, and plunging into the water to follow us as we passed. The sound they utter is something between bellowing and very loud snorting.

    Edward Parry   *An attempt to reach the North Pole*, 1828

The walruses were led by one animal in particular, a much larger and more formidable beast than any of the others . . . His tough hide resisted the entry of the whale lances, which soon bent double. (1818)

    F. W. Beechey   *A voyage towards the North Pole*, 1843

We were very well satisfied not to molest them [walruses], for they would soon have destroyed our boats; but I believe they are never the first to make the attack.

    Edward Parry   *An attempt to reach the North Pole*, 1828

In attacking the walrus in the water the Esquimaux use their gear with much more caution than with the whale, always throwihg the *kateelik* [spear] from some distance, lest the animal should attack the canoe and demolish it with his tusks.

    Edward Parry   *Account of the Esquimaux*, 1826

Wart-hog

Wart-hogs are good diggers, excavating large holes in which they shelter for the night, their heads facing outwards in the best defensive position . . . The animals always went in backwards if there was no room for turning round.

Ernest Neal *Uganda quest,* 1971

Weasel

I can suck melancholy out of a song as a weasel sucks eggs.

William Shakespeare *As you like it, c.* 1599

Leaning over a farm gate (and remaining, of course, perfectly still) I have had a weasel come out of the hedge, sniff around my boots, then place its two forefeet on one of them, peering up as if at my face.

W. Kay Robinson *Britain's beasts of prey,* 1949

When a weasel runs fast on a level hard surface – as across a road – the hinder quarters seem every now and then to jump up as if rebounding from the surface; his legs look too short for the speed he is going.

Richard Jefferies *Wild life in a southern county,* 1879

We came across a weasel dragging an immense object along a tiny trail through the rushes . . . It was a big brown rat. At a guess, I would say that it outweighed the weasel by about ten to one.

Harold Horwood *The foxes of Beachy Cove,* 1967

Happy the weasel in the moonlit churchyard
Twisting a narrow thread
Of life intense between the mounds that hide
The important dead.

James Reeves *Bestiary,* 1949

Weasels frequently hunt in couples, and sometimes more than two will work together. I once saw five and I have heard of eight. The five I saw were working a sandy bank drilled with holes, from which the rabbits in wild alarm were darting in all directions.

Richard Jefferies *The gamekeeper at home,* 1878

The weasel approached cautiously, and the wolf-cub had full opportunity to observe her lean, snake-like body, and her head, erect, eager, and snake-like itself. She came closer and closer. The lean yellow body disappeared for a moment out of the field of his vision. The next moment she was at his throat.

Jack London *White Fang*, 1905
[The wolf-cub is saved by the arrival of his mother.]

There was a weasel lived in the sun
With all his family,
Till a keeper shot him with his gun
And hung him up on a tree,
Where he swings in the wind and rain.

Edward Thomas *The gallows*, 1916

Whale

Strong against tide th'enormous whale
Emerges as he goes.

Christopher Smart *Song to David*, 1763

The largest of all animals, the blue whale, depends for its food on the little shrimp-like krill of Antarctic waters.

Walter Sullivan *Quest for a continent*, 1957

The small crustaceans and molluscs which these animals [whales] chiefly pursue during their polar holiday are most abundant under and between the ice floes.

H. J. Bull *The cruise of the 'Antarctic'*, 1896

Suddenly something behind us blew hard like a swimming horse, and a big whale came up and stared at us, so close that we saw a shine like a polished shoe down through its blowhole. It was so unusual to hear real breathing out at sea, where all living creatures wriggle about silently . . . that we really had a warm family feeling for our old distant cousin the whale.

Thor Heyerdahl *The Kon-Tiki expedition*, 1950

The blue whale is greater in bulk than anything else which is known to have lived on the earth, the weight of the adult being roughly 150 tons.

Walter Sullivan *Quest for a continent*, 1957

Sperm whales have the largest brains in proportion to their body weight of any animal in the world – including man.

Peter Scott   Address to RSPCA, 1981

The Lord had prepared a great fish to swallow up Jonah. And Jonah was in the belly of the fish three days and three nights.

Bible   *Jonah*, 1611

The orca [killer whale] is the only whale that would, or could eat a man . . . There was endless discussion about the Jonah story as orca packs gathered about the ship. The consensus, after examining all authorities available, was that a very large killer might swallow a very small prophet down his gullet with a single gulp, but that the chances of such an event would be quite remote.

Thomas R. Henry   *The white continent*, 1951

A shark fifteen feet in length has been discovered in the stomach of a cachalot [sperm whale]!

Frank T. Bullen   *Cruise of the 'Cachalot'*, 1898

And from the start, by fast degrees,
He won in all hostilities;
Sighted a hammerhead and followed him,
Ripped him from jaw to ventral, swallowed him . . .
Conquered a rorqual in full sight
Of a score of youthful bulls who spurred
Him to the contest, and the fight
Won him the mastery of the herd.

E. J. Pratt   *The Cachalot*, 1926

Wildcat

Wildcats are common animals in the West Highlands [of Scotland] . . . They bear as much relation to the domestic cat as a wolf does to a terrier.

Gavin Maxwell   *Ring of bright water*, 1960

Attempts to make friends with the Scotch wildcat are fruitless . . . But they are so like the ordinary domestic cat that it is hard to believe they are untamable.

Helen M. Sidebotham   *Mysteries of the zoo*, 1927

The fierceness and savage disposition of the wildcat are proverbial, and are displayed even in the kittens, which will spit and hiss vigorously at intruders.

Richard Lydekker in *Harmsworth natural history*, 1910

There is a kind of cat hereof called the wild Cat, which of all things is annoyed with the smell of Rue, and the Almond leafe, and is driven away with that sooner than with any other thing.

John Maplet *A greene forest*, 1567

It would be a pity if the wild cat did become extinct, for although it is admittedly very fierce . . . there is no evidence that it ever springs out on anyone unless it is cornered or if it thinks its kittens are in danger.

W. Kay Robinson *Britain's beasts of prey*, 1949

Wolf

Wake not a sleeping wolf.

William Shakespeare *Henry IV, Pt 2, c.* 1597

HOWLING TO THE MOON

The wolf I've seen . . .
With lurching step around me prowl,
And stop against the moon to howl.

Walter Scott *Marmion*, 1808

The wolf behowls the moon.

William Shakespeare *A midsummer night's dream*, *c.* 1595

The wolf's low whine, prolonged and multiplied,
Possessed the ear of night and over-ruled
All other sounds.

F. W. Faber *Poems*, 1857

The starving wolves along the main sea prowl,
And to the moon in icy valleys howl.

Ambrose Philips *To the earl of Dorset*, 1709

HUNGER AND PURSUIT

The wolf, shivering by the palisade,
nosed the footprints of a hard winter,
grew thin.

  Alfred G. Bailey   *Colonial set*, 1927

The herded wolves, bold only to pursue.

  P. B. Shelley   *Adonais*, 1821

A hungry wolf at all the Herd will run,
In hopes, through many, to make sure of one.

  William Congreve   *Ovid's the art of love*, 1710

The howls, at first distant, drew nearer and nearer. They
came, no doubt, from a pack of the big, almost black, timber-
wolves, which used to go nearly mad with hunger in the very
cold weather, when the caribou roamed about restlessly and
all small animals seemed to have disappeared.

  Harry MacFie and Hans Westerlund   *Wasa-wasa*,
1951

They had entered the northern extension of the Great
American desert, where hardly any game is to be had, and
where 'the very wolves have to lean against the sandbanks to
howl', such is their emaciation from perpetual famine.

  Achilles Daunt   *The three trappers*, 1882

The Assyrian came down like the wolf on the fold.

  Lord Byron   *The destruction of Sennacherib*, 1815

Cruel as death, and hungry as the grave!
Burning for blood! bony, and gaunt, and grim!
Assembling wolves in raging troops descend.

  James Thomson   *The seasons, winter*, 1726

Such rage inflames the Wolf's wild Heart and Eyes
(Robb'd as he thinks unjustly of his prize) . . .
The Shepherd fain himself would he assail,
But Fear above his hunger does prevail.

  Abraham Cowley   *Verses on several occasions*, 1663

The she-wolf was not more than half-a-dozen feet away,
sitting in the snow and wistfully regarding him . . . He knew

it to be the wistfulness of a great hunger. He was the food, and the sight of him excited in her the gustatory sensations. Her mouth opened, the saliva drooled forth.

Jack London   *White Fang*, 1907

The pass was steep and rugged,
The wolves they howled and whined;
But he ran like a whirlwind up the pass,
And he left the wolves behind.

T. B. Macaulay   *The battle of Lake Regillus*, 1842

WOLF LEGENDS

Many accusations [of witchcraft] included that of turning into an animal, or forcing others to do so. The commonest form of this was transformation into a wolf.

Rollo Ahmed   *The black art*, 1936

In 1618 [it was related] a peasant was attacked by a wolf whilst he was hewing timber; he defended himself, and smote off a foreleg of the beast. The moment that the blood began to flow the wolf's form changed, and he recognized a woman without her arm.

S. Baring-Gould   *A book of folklore*, 1913

Virgil and Pliny refer to [as a fact] that he whom the wolf sees before it is itself seen loses his voice.

F. T. Elworthy   *The evil eye*, 1895

In many parts of the world where wolves abound it was forbidden for anyone to speak of them, 'lest the wolves should hear and rend you'.

J. W. Wickwar   *Witchcraft and the black art*, 1925

'When one of the Cernogratz family died here the wolves came from far and near and howled at the edge of the forest just before the death hour . . . At such a time the keepers say there would be scores of them, gliding about in the shadows and howling in chorus.'

'Saki'   *The wolves of Cernogratz*, 1923

[In India] I heard many accounts of babies having been stolen by wolves and reared by them . . . The legend handed down to us by the Conscript Fathers about Romulus and

Remus, which many have ridiculed for twenty-six centuries, may [therefore] well have been true at a time when wolves flourished in the valley of the Tiber.

Viscount Wolseley *The story of a soldier's life*, 1903

THE WOLF DEFENDED

An expert has called for worldwide action to halt the extinction of wolves. Dr Giorgio Boscagli, a senior ecologist, said: 'There's no such thing as a big bad wolf.' He blamed the fairy tale of Little Red Riding Hood for giving wolves a bad name. 'Packs of stray dogs in search of food are the beasts who massacre farm animals.'

Leslie Childe in *Daily Telegraph*, 30 Aug. 1983

A wolf, with hunger fierce and bold,
Ravag'd the plains, and thinn'd the fold . . .
But wolves eat sheep just now and then –
Ten thousands are devour'd by men!

John Gay *Fables*, 1727

There, from the blowing and raining,
Crouching, I sought to hide me.
Something rustled; two green eyes shone;
And a wolf lay down beside me!

His wet fur pressed against me;
Each of us warmed the other;
Each of us felt in the stormy dark
That man and beast were brother.

Bayard Taylor *Collected poems*, 1880

Yak

Yaks are found only at great elevations, ranging in summer from about 14,000 to upwards of 20,000 feet. They are at all times impatient of heat, and delight in cold.

Harmsworth natural history, 1910

On the way down we met a few yaks puffing and steaming in their progress uphill . . . They reminded me of overstuffed ottomans, with fringes of long black hair rather in the shape of loose covers.

Antonia Deacock *No purdah in Padam*, 1960

Their colour is a mixture of white and black and they are very beautiful to the sight . . . Many of these cattle have become domesticated.

Marco Polo   *Travels*, dictated 1298

Never have I seen a more inoffensive-looking beast, with its long hair and mild brown eyes . . . Wood Johnson sat [on it] nonchalantly, but then, with the idea of getting the yak to move, he hit it. The yak did move. From a gentle doormat-like creature it became suddenly possessed of seven devils. It commenced to tear rapidly round and round in circles, and in the middle of one of these circles its back arched bow-like, and Wood Johnson sailed through the air.

F. S. Smythe   *The Kangchenjunga adventure*, 1932

Zebra

From the dark woods that breathe of fallen showers,
Harnessed with level rays in golden reins,
The zebras draw the dawn across the plains,
Wading knee-deep among the scarlet flowers.

Roy Campbell   *The zebras*, 1930

A large herd of zebra came to the pool . . . One young male suddenly went forward, but two of the older males turned on him at once, pushing him with their noses.

Cherry Kearton   *The animals came to drink*, 1932

No one has ever seen a thin zebra, although they are stuffed with parasites; these were no exception. They looked like highly varnished animated toys.

Elspeth Huxley   *The flame trees of Thika*, 1959

The zebra were stolid, keeping their noses to the ground, except for two of their number which kept pace with the herd a little distance on either side – sentinels, always maintaining a watch for danger.

Cherry Kearton   *The animals came to drink*, 1932

Animals in captivity

The more active an animal is in its natural state, the crueller it is to cage it.

  Joan Ward-Harris *Creature comforts*, 1979

Wild things in captivity
while they keep their own wild purity
won't breed, they mope, they die.

  D. H. Lawrence *Pansies*, 1929

In the mid-nineteenth century the great German animal dealer Karl Hagenbeck created an entirely new form of zoological garden. Up until then animals had been stuffed into ill-designed, unsanitary, heavily barred cages . . . Instead of grim, iron-barred dungeons, he gave his animals light and space.

  Gerald Durrell *Beasts in my belfry*, 1973

'Nothing will make me believe that an acre or two of concrete enclosure will make up to a wolf or tiger-cat for the range of night prowling that would belong to it in a wild state. Think of the dictionary of sound and scent and recollection that unfolds before a real wild beast as it comes out from its lair every evening.'

  'Saki' *The mappined life*, 1923

Many of the natural thickets had been cleared to prevent obstruction of view, and the topography was not unlike that of lion country in Kenya, with its grasslands, woods, streams and hillocks. The Lions of Longleat . . . would be seen in something very close to their natural surroundings.

  Mary Chipperfield *Lions on the lawn*, 1971

There are many things to be remembered when making friends with the animals in the Zoo. In the first place they dislike gloves, and a gloved hand is far more likely to be bitten than a naked one.

Helen M. Sidebotham   *Mysteries of the zoo*, 1927

It was rather like watching an animal performing on a music-hall stage. One always tells oneself that the animal likes it, and one always knows that it doesn't.

'Saki'   *The unbearable Bassington*, 1912

Does anyone really believe . . . that being bumped and hauled around the countryside for ever in a cage and then laughed and screamed at by a thousand human faces is not both physical and mental torture for a wild animal?

David Jacobs   in *RSPCA Today*, autumn, 1979

Some were wild animals, and some came from the circus . . . These were very, very cowed and afraid, and they never once wanted to do any of their tricks.

Tippi Hedren   quoted in *Telegraph Sunday Magazine*, 18 Dec. 1983
[See The animal world, p. 3]

Making animals perform for the amusement of human beings is
Utterly disgraceful and abominable.
Animals are animals and have their nature
And that's enough, it is enough, leave it alone.

Stevie Smith   *Collected poems*, 1975

BEAR

Bears have been trained for many centuries and yet they remain one of the species of animals which humans know least about, for they never show what they are thinking.

Antony Hippisley-Coxe   *A seat at the circus*, 1951

The bear is the most dangerous animal on the circus . . . Nevertheless, he is very easy to teach, seems to have a sense of humour and an instinct for buffoonery, and is amusing to watch.

Ruth Manning-Sanders   *The English circus*, 1952

My mother saw a dancing bear
By the schoolyard, a day in June.
The keeper stood with chain and bar
And whistle-pipe, and played a tune.

   Charles Causley   *Collected poems*, 1975

We are told all things were made for man . . .
Therefore as thou wert born,
Bruin, for man, and man makes nothing of thee
In any other way, most logically,
It follows that thou must be born to dance,
That that great snout of thine was formed on purpose
To hold a ring.

   Robert Southey   *The dancing bear*, 1829
   [Southey is, of course, writing ironically.]

Slender: You are afraid if you see the bear loose, are you not?
Anne: Ay, indeed, sir.
Slender: That's meat and drink to me, now. I have seen
Sackerson loose twenty times and have taken him by the
chain.

   William Shakespeare   *The merry wives of Windsor*,
   c. 1600
   [Sackerson was a famous bear exhibited at Southwark.]

The puritan hated bear-baiting not because it gave pain to the
bear, but because it gave pleasure to the spectator.

   T. B. Macaulay   *History of England*, 1848–55
   [Whatever the motive, the hatred could be regarded as a step
   in the right direction.]

CAMEL

In dreams I see the Dromedary still,
As once in a gay park I saw him stand . . .
He blinked upon the rabble lazily;
And still some trace of majesty forlorn
And a coarse grace remained: his head was high,
Though his gaunt flanks with a great mange were worn.
There was not any yearning in his eye,
But on his lips and nostrils infinite scorn.

   A. Y. Campbell   *Poems*, 1926

Big Bill was standing in the middle of the paddock
ruminating, and as I got near him I greeted him . . . Big Bill's
jaws stopped moving and his pale yellow eyes fastened on me.
Then he suddenly stepped forward swiftly, his head lunged
down with open mouth and he sank his long discoloured
teeth into the clothing on my chest, lifted me off my feet,
shook me, and dropped me.

Gerald Durrell *Beasts in my belfry*, 1973

CHIMPANZEE

Anyone watching our Cameroons chimpanzee Missie sitting
at table in her salon, pouring out three cups of coffee one
after the other, and then smoking a cigarette, having lighted it
herself, must have had an uncontrollable urge to laugh. But
she also gave food for thought.

Ludwig Heck *Bobby the chimpanzee and other
friends*, 1931

I handed him the cigarette packet. He opened it, took out a
cigarette, and put it between his lips. He then reached out his
hand again and I gave him the matches; to my astonishment
he took one out of the box, struck it, lit the cigarette, and
threw the box down on the table.

Gerald Durrell *The new Noah*, 1972

In one of the American monkey stations a completely tame
and highly 'civilized' chimpanzee named Jojo always
switched the light off itself before settling down to sleep.

Hermann Dembeck *Willingly to school*, 1970

He shared, I am happy to say, Durrell's bed and not mine, so
it was essential that he was trained not to wet the bed. After
one or two false starts he did learn to hang his nether regions
over the side of the bed whenever he wanted to spend a
penny, although in his enthusiasm he sometimes failed to
make it.

Jacquie Durrell *Beasts in my bed*, 1967

The four chimpanzees squabble at times, but the keeper,
after separating the combatants, makes them shake hands;
and now, whenever Jack has a fight on his conscience, he

rushes up to his late enemy and offers to shake hands as soon as he hears the keeper's voice.

Helen M. Sidebotham *Mysteries of the zoo*, 1927

The chimpanzee possesses a certain sense of humour . . . When the animal has succeeded in overturning a pail of water and caused a great deal of this, often including the pail, to descend upon the head of some poor unfortunate human attendant, it will clap both its hands over the top of its own head and emit a succession of loud, explosive noises from its larynx.

R. H. Smythe *How animals talk*, 1959

The two orangs have a habit of stretching out their hands to greet visitors. As soon as a lady or gentleman accepts the outstretched hand, she or he involuntarily leans forward a little towards the bars – and in a flash the chimpanzee darts down, grabs whatever he has set his sights on, and carries off his spoils.

Karl Hagenbeck *Beasts and men*, 1909

Miss Brewer tells how she taught the two chimps to feed for themselves, even going so far as catching and eating termites to show how it was done.

Daily Telegraph, 28 Jan. 1978

ELEPHANT

Once tamed, the elephant becomes the gentlest and most obedient of all creatures; it becomes devoted to its keeper, displaying great affection for him, anticipating his wishes, and seeming to guess what will please him.

Comte de Buffon *Natural history*, 1749–88

The famous Jumbo, sold to America by the London Zoo, firmly refused to go into a travelling box until his keeper, for whom he had a great affection, went in first.

Helen M. Sidebotham *Mysteries of the zoo*, 1927

The elephant took and gave me my money – took off my hat – opened a door, *trunked* a whip – and behaved so well that I wish he was my butler.

Lord Byron *Letters*, 1833

Lord BYRON & Elephant.

A lady asked Harry Houdini why he didn't revive his famous Vanishing Elephant. Harry, deadpan, explained that the U.S. President, Herbert Hoover, had ruled that elephants should be conserved. 'I made two disappear a day, that is twelve a week. Mr Hoover said that I was exhausting the elephant supply!'

Milbourne Christopher *Houdini*, 1969

He stands with his forefeet on the drum
and the other, the old one, the pallid hoary female
must creep her great bulk beneath the bridge of him.

On her knees, in utmost caution
all agog, and curling up her trunk
she edges through without upsetting him.

D. H. Lawrence *Two performing elephants*, 1929

The fair is now broke, but it is allowed still to sell animals there. Therefore, if any lady or gentleman have occasion for a tame elephant, let him enquire of Mr Pinkethman, who has one to dispose of at a reasonable rate.

The Tatler, 24 May 1709

GIBBON

The gibbons live on an island in one of the lakes, and Bimbo was somewhat notorious for his prodigious leaping ability between the trees. One day a visitor caught his eye, and Bimbo jumped over more than fifteen feet of water and chased the poor man until he found refuge in the Gents' lavatory.

Terry Murphy *Some of my best friends are animals*, 1979
[Director of the Dublin Zoo.]

GIRAFFE

It [a young giraffe] was brought up with the warden's own children and played with them every day . . . Finally he was taken off to a herd of wild giraffe that had recently come into the park. But one look was sufficient. The small brain was quite unable to register the fact that such extraordinary animals could exist, and that he was one of them: he turned and bolted.

Alan Moorehead *No room in the ark*, 1959

When we had giraffes separated from the public only by high railings, they would be forever leaning over and taking food from people; and this was dangerous. You can lose a lot of animals from the wrong food or even too much of the right food.

Terry Murphy   *Some of my best friends are animals*, 1979

HIPPOPOTAMUS

At one time we had a hippo called Harry in our circus . . . He loved human company, and I had often been in the habit of visiting him for a chat. Harry was not very bright but otherwise was a real pet – all one and a half tons of him. He liked to have his nose rubbed and his head stroked.

Mary Chipperfield   *Lions on the lawn*, 1971

To the hippos' friends the familiarity of tickling the insides of their mouths is allowed; whereas if a stranger took this liberty his hand would be badly trapped.

Helen M. Sidebotham   *Mysteries of the zoo*, 1927

JAGUAR

My own first impression of a living jaguar was not one of pure pleasure . . . He moved up and down the floor of his cage with a tread noiseless as the flight of an owl. At each step I took towards him he shrank from me, flattening his ears and disclosing his white teeth, while his shining pale and yellow eyes partially closed and averted themselves from my sight. For it is his instinct to remain always hidden from the eye, and it confuses and maddens him to be held in place by bars and gazed openly at.

W. H. Hudson   in *Harmsworth natural history*, 1910

LEOPARD

The showman entered the leopard's cage with a light whip in one hand and a hoop in the other. The animals leaped over the whip, through the hoop, and over the man's back, exhibiting as much docility as cats or dogs.

Thomas Frost   *Circus life and circus celebrities*, 1875

. . . the bang of a whip
Brought the animals lolloping onto their chairs (a tail
Hung long and twitching, talking its own thoughts).

Bernard Spencer *The leopards*, 1963

The leopards, who bear the reputation of being less trustful
and more treacherous, have at all times shown great
willingness to make friends at once with anyone.

James Walton *My wild friends*, 1954

LION

The lion-tamer begins by taking the feeding of them into his
own hands . . . Getting to handle the lion, the tamer begins
by stroking him down the back, gradually working up to the
head, which he begins to scratch, and the lion, which, like a
cat, likes friction, begins to rub his head against the hand.
When this familiarity is well established, a board is handed in
to the trainer, which he places across the den and teaches the
lion to jump over it.

A lion-tamer quoted in **Thomas Frost**, *Circus life
and circus celebrities*, 1875

At the proper moment came the roar of the lions, done by an
ingenious instrument contrived for the purpose in case the
lions should not roar when they were wanted to do so.

'Lord' George Sanger *Seventy years a showman*, 1926
[Sanger, 1827–1911, was a well-known circus proprietor.]

The live lion invariably roared on schedule. Not because he
had been trained, but as a protesting reaction to a jolt of
electricity sent through a metal plate on the floor of the
hidden cage . . . Lafayette paid a fine for the inhumane
treatment of the animal but did not change the routine.

Milbourne Christopher *The illustrated history of
magic*, 1973
[Lafayette was an American magician of the early twentieth
century.]

At the Grand Opera House in Indianapolis the lion seized
one of the magician's pet dogs which had slipped through the
bars of the cage. Armed with a pistol containing a single
round of blank ammunition, Lafayette went to the rescue.

The lion dropped the dog, sprang at the illusionist, and knocked him unconscious to the floor.

Milbourne Christopher *The illustrated history of magic,* 1973

Although cars and people are fully covered by insurance, up to £100,000, the park is as safe as houses. Our peacocks are more liable to do damage than Mr Chipperfield's lions . . . Nor are they as melodic and tuneful as our lions, which, as you can hear, give out a friendly roar of welcome – a roar more soothing than frightening. I'm all for having lions around the place.

Marquess of Bath, at the opening of the lion reserve at Longleat, 3 Apr. 1966

Nobody was eaten here today! The first safari into the lion's compound [at Longleat] was watched with disdain by all of the lions in the pride . . . The 46 lions already here roam at will beneath the trees in the compound, laze on the verandahs of their insulated shelters, or pace up and down inside the fence.

The Times, 4 Apr. 1966

Just like human babies, cubs like something to cuddle . . . Someone brought in a brightly coloured alarm clock one day for the cook to use and it lay on the floor for a bit, where Marquis discovered it during one of his perambulations. Its tick fascinated him, and he had soon lain down on top of it and gone to sleep. From then on, the alarm clock, always ticking its comfort, was his constant cuddly companion.

Mary Chipperfield *Lions on the lawn,* 1971
[The little lion cub was brought up at Longleat by the daughter of the famous circus proprietor.]

Poor prisoner in a cage,
I understand your rage . . .
Better, perhaps, be dead
Than locked in this dark den;
Forgive us, lion, then
Who did not ever choose
Our circuses and zoos.

Leonard Clark *Lion*

I remember sharing the last of my moist buns with a boy and a lion . . . Wild as seed-cake, ferocious as a hearthrug, the depressed and verminous lion nibbled like a mouse at his half a bun.

Dylan Thomas *Quite early one morning*, 1954

I once sat up two days and two nights with a sick lion, and managed to save his life by putting mustard-plasters on his chest.

'Lord' George Sanger *Seventy years a showman*, 1926

Pezon [a famous French lion tamer] admitted that he never dared take his eyes off those of his lions until he contrived to have some highly-charged electric wires between them and him.

C. J. Cornish *Animals today*, 1898

Macarthy was lying in the centre of the cage, with the lion which had first attacked him still biting and tearing him. Discharges of blank cartridge being found ineffectual, the heated iron was applied to the lion's nose, and it then released him.

Thomas Frost *Circus life and circus celebrities*, 1875
[Macarthy was a lion-tamer who had excited his lions in a foolish mimic 'lion-hunt'.]

A lion was imported here at the fair . . . I saw him embrace his keeper with his paws, and lick his face. Others saw him receive the man's head in his mouth, and restore it to him again unhurt. We advised the honest man to discontinue the practice – a practice hardly reconcilable to prudence, unless he had a head to spare.

William Cowper *Letters*, 1778

MONKEY

Those who buy monkeys from dealers and find that, instead of getting the angelic creatures they imagined, they have purchased mischievous little imps, are only too pleased to offer their mistakes to the London Zoo.

Helen M. Sidebotham *Mysteries of the zoo*, 1927

The monkeys [at the Zoo] stared back at the expectant crowds with their old, sad eyes. It seemed just a matter of luck which side of the bars you were.

Colin Howard   in *Evening News*, 28 Aug. 1948

Two little creatures
With faces the size of
A pair of pennies
Are clasping each other.
'Ah, do not leave me,'
One says to the other,
In the high monkey-
Cage in the beast-shop.

Padraic Colum   *Monkeys*, 1932

Wanda was bored. So my mother (who always believed the devil would find work for idle hands to do) taught her to knit and to sew. She would sit for hours, making monumental stitches in pieces of cloth or pulling the wool laboriously round her knitting needles.

Buster Lloyd-Jones   *The animals came in one by one*, 1966

The act of throwing projectiles has not been given to the brute creation . . . Inspect the Zoological Gardens, where there is a charming show of monkeys, and I will stake my ears that you will never see one of them do that which we commonly call throwing a stone.

Charles Waterton   *Essays on natural history*, 1857

PANDA

I have never had any illusions about pandas being cuddly teddy-bears. Although not bears, giant pandas have the weight, compactness, and powerful bite of a bear the size of, say, the Himalayan black. Such a creature can easily mangle a man if it has a mind to.

David Taylor   *Next panda, please*, 1982

[Chi-Chi] provided ample copy for Fleet Street by escaping twice from her enclosure. On the first occasion she climbed over a low fence . . . On the second, she scrambled out of her large pit while warm water was being tipped into her now famous tub.

Ramona and Desmond Morris *The giant panda*, 1981

The hopes and beliefs that the two giant pandas would fall in love resulted in the most extravagant arrangements . . . But never at any time were the prospects even hopeful. Chi-Chi and An-An ignored each other completely.

James Alldiss *Animals as friends*, 1973
[Chi-Chi was from the London Zoo, An-An from Moscow. Alldiss was head keeper at the former.]

RODENT

During the next few days census papers will be issued to every section of the London Zoo . . . In the Rodent House the birth-rate is so high that the keeper is likely to find that a new family has arrived overnight.

Daily Telegraph, 19 Dec. 1938

TIGER

They trapped her in the Indian hills
And put her in a box; and though so young,
The dockers quailed to hear her voice
As she made war on every bolt and thong.

Clifford Dyment *The tigress*, 1944

I went to the Tower with [a person] who plays on the German flute. He began playing near four or five lions . . . A tiger in the same den started up, leaped over the lion's back, turned and ran under his belly, leaped over him again, and so to and fro incessantly.

John Wesley *Journal*, c. 1739

During these morning talks I had with him, Paul was so avuncular that it was only with difficulty that I remembered he *could* be dangerous if he wanted to be; he would curve his huge head against the bars and let me scratch his ears, purring loudly, so that he seemed more like a giant domestic cat than the popular conception of a bloodthirsty tiger. He would accept my gifts of meat with regal condescension.

Gerald Durrell   *Beasts in my belfry*, 1973
[Durrell was working at Whipsnade Open-air Zoo.]

Helen Blight, the daughter of a musician in the circus band . . . was performing with the animals at Greenwich Fair one day, when a tiger exhibited some sullenness or waywardness, for which she very imprudently struck it with a whip. The infuriated beast sprang at her with a hoarse roar, seized her by the throat, and killed her.

Thomas Frost   *Circus life and circus celebrities*, 1875

A menagerie is a dismal and disgusting spectacle; if anybody wants to see a mangy tiger pacing interminably round a tiny prison under the ceaseless provocation of the staring, tittering humans, he must have an extraordinary and deplorable taste in fun.

Ivor Brown   *Farewell to the fair* in *Modern essays and sketches*, ed. J. W. Marriott, 1935

Mr Goodbeare could remember
When the escaped and hungering tiger
Flickered lithe and fierce through Foxton Wood.

Osbert Sitwell   *Elegy for Mr Goodbeare*, 1927

Tigers are affectionate if they take to you at all, but never demonstrative in the way of lions. When he came out of the water after a swim, Kumar would give me one lick with his rough tongue and would then settle down with a bone he had invariably brought with him.

Mary Chipperfield   *Lions on the lawn*, 1971

Mothers of large families, who claim to common sense,
Will find a Tiger well repay the trouble and expense.

Hilaire Belloc   *Bad child's book of beasts*, 1896

There was a young lady of Riga
Who went for a ride on a tiger:
They returned from the ride
With the lady inside,
And a smile on the face of the tiger.

Anon.

WOLF

Most days of the week he would harness up the wolves and take them for a tour of the gardens . . . Afterwards he would sit for anything up to an hour in their cage. I once saw him flat on his back with two sets of wet slobbering jaws inches from his throat, but he was so much at ease that he asked me the time.

James Alldiss *Animals as friends*, 1973
[This gentleman received special permission from the London Zoo to enjoy the company of his lupine friends.]

I encountered four wolves bounding along a side-walk, reined by an old Fellow who gives them their morning run. But could he hold them? Rather to my surprise it was they, not I, who crept under a seat.

G. W. Stonier *Pictures on the pavement*, 1955

Index